First edition copyright © 2021 by Melody Tyden

This edition copyright © 2024 by Melody Tyden

All rights reserved.

The characters and events portrayed in this book are fictitious. Any similarity to real persons, living or dead, is coincidental and not intended by the author.

No part of this book may be reproduced, or stored in a retrieval system, or transmitted in any form or by any means, electronic, mechanical, photocopying, recording, or otherwise, without express written permission of the publisher.

Cover design by: Aisling Elizabeth

Figuring It Out

MELODY TYDEN

Contents

Playlist	1
1. Chapter One	3
2. Chapter Two	19
3. Chapter Three	39
4. Chapter Four	47
5. Chapter Five	61
6. Chapter Six	75
7. Chapter Seven	95
8. Chapter Eight	109
9. Chapter Nine	123
10. Chapter Ten	135
11. Chapter Eleven	151
12. Chapter Twelve	165
13. Epilogue	179
Bonus Scene	189
Keep in Touch	191

Playlist (Amy & Austin)

- **Whatever It Takes** - Lifehouse
- **Back to You** - Selena Gomez
- **Coming Home** - Kaiser Chiefs
- **To Make You Feel My Love** - Adele
- **Back to December** - Taylor Swift
- **Don't Stop Believin'** - Journey
- **Believer** - Imagine Dragons
- **The Dance** - Garth Brooks

Chapter One

~**Amelia**~

As I pulled on my skates in the coach's dressing room, I had to resist the urge to stop and pinch myself. When I got assigned to profile my ex-ice dance partner, Austin Black, for a magazine article, I could never have imagined that it would lead to me choreographing a new program for him and his new partner, Grace Matthews. In a few months, they would perform that program in front of a worldwide audience at the Olympics, and if people liked it, it could lead to a whole new career path that I'd never considered before.

After the accident that stopped me from training, and everything that followed which ultimately ended my skating career, I never thought I'd return to the world of elite figure skating. Choreography might be different from competing, but it was still an amazing opportunity, and I intended to make the most of it.

Every time someone walked in the room, I looked up, my body tensing involuntarily, and Brian, Austin and Grace's coach, noticed. "Are you expecting somebody?"

"I've been wondering when Mrs Black is going to find me," I answered honestly.

Hurricane Cynthia, as I'd heard her referred to by other coaches in the past, was Austin's mom, and far from my biggest fan. Since joining Austin and Grace's team, I hadn't seen her at the rink, and it felt like waiting for a bomb to drop. I would rather get the confrontation over with than keep on wondering when she might appear.

"You're in luck," Brian replied, looking completely unsurprised by my confession. "She's taking a break from the rink."

His words surprised me, but maybe they shouldn't have. After my confrontation with my own mother over the lies she told that kept me and Austin apart, I suspected that Austin and his mom must have had a similar showdown. If Austin felt even half as betrayed as I did, he might have told her to stay away.

"How are you feeling in general?" Brian asked, keeping up an easy conversation as I tied my laces. "You have everything under control with school and your commitments here?"

Along with devoting hours a day to working with Austin and Grace, I still had my university journalism program and my magazine internship to keep up with, but I was determined to make it work. "I've spoken to my professors and my internship supervisor. They're willing to make some accommodations as long as I keep them updated and ask for help when I need it."

"Good. We're glad you're here, Mia."

Together, the two of us headed out to the rink where the hour and a half session flew by while I worked on some new step sequences with Austin and Grace. Almost before I knew it, we were stepping off the ice again, and Austin gently took my elbow to move me to the side.

"What are you up to for the rest of the day?"

Those were the first words either of us had said all day that weren't related to skating. After our emotional conversation the day before, I still felt a bit tender and exposed, and I imagined he did too.

"I've got an assignment for one of my classes due tomorrow, so I'm meeting up with some friends to work on it. What about you?"

"Gym training, and another on-ice session this afternoon." His gaze darted over to Grace, as if checking she couldn't hear him before he spoke again. "Do you want to have lunch in the bar before you go? There are still a few more things we need to talk about."

After everything we'd said the day before, I didn't know exactly what could be left to go over, but I agreed anyway. "Sure. Let me go change and I'll meet you there."

~**Austin**~

The sports bar at the club usually had a smaller crowd than the cafeteria, which was why I chose it for lunch with Amy. I didn't want our lunch to feel rushed or too public when the topic I wanted to discuss couldn't have been more personal. We'd talked about a lot of things the day before, but not everything. One important thing still had to be cleared up and I didn't want to put it off any longer.

Amy arrived a couple of minutes after me, sinking down into the seat across from me, having discarded the coat and scarf she wore on the ice. Without them, I could see the wide V-neck shirt she wore and the four-leaf clover shining against her skin, just below her collarbone.

The fact that she still wore the necklace suggested it meant a lot to her, giving me hope that I still meant something to her too.

I just had to figure out what that something might be.

"How are you doing?" I asked as she took a long drink of water from the glass I'd already ordered for her.

Though I left the question neutral and vague, she knew what I meant: how did she feel about everything after our intense conversation and the things we'd learned?

She didn't waste any time getting straight into it. "I talked to my parents about what happened after the accident."

"How did that go?" Based on the conversation I had with my mom, I suspected hers wouldn't have been much fun either.

Her grimace confirmed that suspicion. "Not well. My dad asked me to apologize to you. He said he's sorry he didn't stick up for you more when you tried to see me."

Another wave of sadness and regret hit me with the memory of that long-ago day in the hospital but I did my best to push it away. No dwelling on things that couldn't be changed; we'd agreed on that the day before.

"I appreciate that," I replied, keeping my tone even. "Did you talk to your mom too?"

Amy winced again. "Yeah. I got pretty upset with her. Not that she didn't deserve it, but being harsh at this point doesn't change anything. We're going to have to find a way to get past it eventually, and we will, but it's going to be weird between us for a while, I think."

"Yeah, I haven't really talked to my mom since she told me what happened either."

"Our moms kind of suck," Amy said, glancing down at the menu in front of her.

"Totally suck," I amended. "Like vacuums on steroids."

Her eyes jumped back up to me, startled, and when I smiled, we both laughed. A sad, slightly sour laugh, perhaps, but a laugh all the same. It felt good to share it with her.

After placing our order, I leaned forward, my elbows on the table, and got to the real reason I asked her to have lunch with me. "I know this conversation is four years late and a lot has changed since then, but we never got to talk about what happened the night before the accident. At Ben's party. Or rather, after the party, when I took you home."

"When you kissed me," she added softly.

"Right. When I kissed you." My gaze dropped to her lips as I said the words. Even after four years, I could still remember the way they felt pressed against mine. "I owe you the explanation I never got a chance to give you."

"I have wondered about it," she admitted, a light blush tinting her cheeks. "It was so out of character for you."

If she really thought that, I'd obviously done a much better job of hiding my feelings than I realized.

"That's the thing, Amy: it wasn't out of character at all. I'd been wanting to kiss you for a really long time before that night, I just always managed to hold myself back before."

Her eyebrows drew tightly together, making her glasses fall down her nose. She pushed them back up, her curious gaze never wavering. "I don't understand. You were never interested in me."

If only that were true. "I *was* interested. Very interested. I just didn't tell you about it."

"Why would you want to hide it?"

"Because I convinced myself that it was wrong for me to feel that way about you when you were so much younger than me. I thought I needed to wait until you were older."

"But you aren't that much older than me."

She sounded so unsure that I realized I must not have been making things clear enough, and I tried to speak even more plainly.

"It doesn't seem like anything now, when you're 20 and I'm 23, but at the time, it felt like a really big deal. I certainly thought so, anyway. I forced myself to hold back because of your age but I liked you, Amy. A lot." I studied her face, her pale blue eyes behind her glasses, her blushing cheeks and her expressive mouth that twitched in uncertainty. "You really didn't have any idea?"

She shook her head, an almost wistful smile flashing across those lips I'd just been staring at. "None. But I... I liked you too, Austin. A lot."

From the way she kissed me back that night, I hoped she felt the same but I never knew for sure. Even four years later, it felt incredible to hear her confirm it.

"That's partly why it hurt so much..." she started, but I didn't let her finish, knowing exactly what she was about to say.

"...when I thought you didn't want to see me again."

We both smiled, a smile of commiseration and understanding. Knowing that she had been hurting the same way I had made me feel somehow better and worse at the same time.

"When you came here as Mia, I felt something for you then too," I continued. "You already know that. I wasn't exactly subtle about it. Now that I know that you were her, that she's you, I can't pretend I see you as just another choreographer. Maybe things have changed. Maybe *we've* changed and we don't have that connection anymore, but maybe we're still the same people at heart and we still do. I don't know about you, but I want to find out for sure."

Her eyes dropped to the table, shielding her emotions from me, and I tried to give her a moment. Maybe I shouldn't have blurted it all out quite so bluntly, but I'd had enough of keeping my feelings a secret. Losing her the way I did put a lot of things into perspective, and now that she'd returned, I didn't want to make the same mistakes again.

If we didn't end up together this time, it wouldn't be because I didn't tell her how I felt.

Despite my best efforts to wait for a response, her silence unnerved me, and I couldn't help giving her a gentle prompt. "What do you think, Amy? What do you want to do next?"

Before I could stop myself, I reached over and took her glasses off, pulling them gently from her face so I could see her the way I remembered her. Her eyes darted back up to me in surprise, and closed briefly as my fingers brushed against her face.

When they opened, however, the look in those pretty eyes made my stomach sink. It looked like resignation, and the Amy I knew never gave up on what she wanted. If she was giving up now, maybe she didn't want me after all.

"Austin, working on your program is an incredible opportunity for me."

I blinked at her, trying to make sense of her words. I didn't care about the program; I wanted to talk about us.

"I'm really glad that we had this talk," she continued. "I don't want there to be any more secrets or misunderstandings between us, but..."

That 'but' landed hard on my heart, and I had a feeling what might be coming next before she said it.

"... I also think that we don't need any distractions, either of us. You've got so much riding on this year, and things between us, whatever they are, have never been simple. I think it's probably best that we keep things professional. Friendly professional, I mean. We can talk and share things, but for now, I think we should leave it at that."

Frustratingly, I could see her point. I'd been telling myself the same thing all year.

No distractions. Stick to the goal.

But the other thing I knew, the thing I had learned from everything that happened with her, was not to let chances pass me by, and that moment felt a lot like her slipping through my fingers again.

"Do you still feel something for me?" I asked her straight out, with no further build-up. If she said no, I could agree to what she suggested, but if even a chance existed that there might be something more there, I intended to fight for it.

She struggled with her answer for a moment before finally looking back at me. "Of course I do. But..."

"No buts," I interrupted. "That was all I wanted to know."

"Austin, listen..."

"I heard you, so now you can listen to me. It's been an intense few days, and for the next few weeks, we're going to be working together pretty closely. If you want to stick to being 'friendly professional' for now, that's fine. But once the program is ready, once we go to Japan for our first competition with it, I want to give this a proper chance. Will you agree to that?"

Even though her lips tightened, I could see her conviction weakening. "If I agree, will it make things weird between us? Or between you and Grace? I don't want to come between you, especially now."

"Grace is my skating partner and nothing more. She gets no say in who I'm interested in. Come on, Amy. I'm not asking for a lifetime commitment here. Just that, a month from now, you might go on a date with me."

A laugh bubbled out of her before she covered her mouth in that gesture I remembered so well, making sure that she didn't snort. My heart swelled with affection as I watched her.

"Alright," she agreed, giving me a sweet, small smile. "When we get to Japan, we'll see how it goes. And in the meantime, we focus on your program."

"You mean *your* program."

Her smile widened, and in that smile, I saw *my* Amy, the one who always appreciated me having her back.

When she smiled that way, the whole world seemed brighter, and I wanted to live in that world all the time. Every second spent with her only strengthened that certainty, and after everything we'd been through to get to that point, I would do everything I could to find a way to make it happen.

~Amelia~

The next day found me back at the rink for another session with Austin and Grace, determined to keep things between us professional, just like I told him I wanted to.

It wouldn't be easy after finding out he had feelings for me back when we were skating together.

The admission surprised and flattered me. Even after he kissed me, the thought had honestly never crossed my mind that he might have been harbouring long-term feelings for me, the same as I had for him. It would have seemed too much like wish fulfillment, too good to be true, and I'd always been too realistic to believe in fairy tales.

But despite the ego boost his confession gave me, in the end, it didn't change anything. No matter how much we wanted to, we couldn't turn back time and save ourselves from all the heartbreak we'd been through. We could only look ahead, and for the time being, that meant focusing on the program I needed to create for them. I couldn't allow anything to distract either him or me from that goal.

The session that afternoon went as well as I could have hoped. With every minute we spent together, Grace trusted me a little more, slowly starting to believe that I genuinely wanted to know what felt right and comfortable for her, and trusting that I only wanted to make her look good. We were working on individual elements to start with since the program still hadn't taken its final shape in my head, but I wanted to start working through the whole thing with them soon. We only had a little over three weeks to go before the first competition where they would perform it, so the next few weeks were going to be intense.

Along with mastering the individual moves, they needed to convey the story of the program, and for that, they needed to understand my vision for it. With that in mind, I asked them a question when we all got off the ice at the end of the session. "Are you guys busy tonight?"

They shook their heads almost in unison and Austin answered first. "I don't have any plans. Why?"

"The program I'm envisioning is based on a movie, but I want to be sure that you feel a connection with the story and that you think you can portray it. I'd like for us all to watch it together."

Austin's wistful smile suggested that he remembered the last movie we watched together as well as I did. The last program I created for us had been based on a movie too, and we watched it at my house after the awkward dinner at his mom's place. Even though my parents were in the next room and we didn't even sit on the same couch, it still felt almost romantic to be sitting alone with him, watching a romantic movie. Every time the characters on screen kissed, my cheeks flushed as I imagined what it would feel like if it were Austin and me instead.

At the time, I hoped he wouldn't notice my blush or guess my thoughts, but after his revelation at lunch the day before, I wondered if he'd been thinking the same thing at the time.

Was he thinking about it now?

"That's fine with me," he said, not giving me any clue about what else might be going on in his head.

"Me too," Grace agreed. "Austin's place is pretty comfortable, we could go there."

An annoying twinge of jealousy tugged at my chest at the thought that she knew what Austin's house was like, that she'd been there before. Although Austin told me he was interested in me and not her, they still had four years of history as partners that I hadn't been a part of.

Austin's lips tightened momentarily at Grace's words, and I thought for a moment he might refuse, but instead, he nodded after a short pause. "Sure, I'm happy to host. Do you want me to come pick you up, Amy?"

Though most people had adjusted to calling me Mia, Austin still called me Amy, and it didn't seem worth my time to keep correcting him.

Grace's eyes widened at his offer to pick me up and I quickly shook my head. Him showing me any kind of preferential treatment that would upset Grace was exactly what I *didn't* want and why I insisted that we keep things professional. "No, don't worry, I'll get there. Just send me the address. Is seven o'clock okay?"

We all agreed on the details and Austin promised to text me his address. I waved a quick goodbye to them before getting changed out of my skates and heading back to campus to get to my next class. Despite the demands of choreographing their new program, I still had my university classes to attend and my internship at the magazine to complete.

If I made it through the next few weeks without dropping any of the balls I was juggling, it would be a miracle.

By the time my class ended and I'd done some work on my assignments, dinner time had arrived, and I met my friends in the school cafeteria. As soon as I sat down with my food, Rosa pounced on me.

"Okay, spill it, Mia. What's going on? You look like you swallowed some sunshine."

They hadn't seen me the day before since I'd worked late at the magazine and grabbed supper there. How she knew in just a few minutes that something had happened, I didn't understand, but since only one thing could account for my good mood, I confessed the truth to them.

"I talked to Austin yesterday and he told me that he was interested in me back when we skated together."

"Romantically interested?" Rosa pressed, and when I nodded, she squealed in delight. "I knew it! Isn't that what I always said?"

She looked around the table for validation and we all had to acknowledge that she had, in fact, always insisted that he liked me.

"And what about now?" Jenna asked, leaning forward curiously. "You said he *was* interested, but what about now?"

"He's kind of still interested," I mumbled, feeling a bit shy about even saying the words out loud. I could still hardly believe any of that conversation actually happened. In so many ways, hearing him say those words had been a dream come true, but I knew all too well what it felt like to have everything I ever wanted right within my grasp and have it all pulled away.

I didn't know if I could survive having that happen again, especially if it happened with Austin.

Of course my friends had questions and by the time I finished answering them and glanced down at my watch, my stomach sank. Sometime, an hour had disappeared. Saying a hurried goodbye to my friends, I sent Austin a quick text to apologize for keeping him and Grace waiting and promising I wouldn't be any later than 7:30.

The taxi dropped me off outside Austin's house at 7:27. The small house on the south side of Forest Hill, a rather ritzy neighbourhood, wasn't far from the skating club. When he sent me the address, he added a disclaimer that he didn't live in the fancy part of Forest Hill, but his house looked comfortable and well-kept. I always knew that his family didn't have to worry about money for skating, but beyond that, I had no idea about his financial situation.

If we were actually going to pursue a relationship at the end of all of this, we still had a lot to learn about each other, as the adults we were now instead of the teenagers we'd been.

After ringing the doorbell, I readied myself to apologize in person for my tardiness, but Grace opened the door instead of Austin.

"Hi Mia, come on in." She gave me a smile that seemed friendly enough, but I couldn't help feeling a little irritated at her acting like the gatekeeper to Austin's house and how comfortable she seemed to be there.

When did I get so jealous? I had to figure out a way to bring that envy under control, especially when I was the one insisting that Austin and I stay professional.

"Thanks, Grace. I'm sorry I'm late."

"It's no problem," she said with a wave of her hand. "Austin and I were just talking. We barely even noticed the time."

I gritted my teeth, forcing myself not to take the bait she dangled in front of me. "Well, I'm here now, so let's go get started."

FIGURING IT OUT

~Austin~

When the doorbell finally rang, I exhaled a relieved sigh. Grace had shown up nearly half an hour ahead of the agreed meeting time while Amy ended up being half an hour late, leaving Grace and I alone together for a long hour of painfully dry conversation. Hanging out with Grace had never been anything like spending time with Amy, where it always felt like we didn't have enough time to get through everything we had to say. Even when I spent the whole day with Amy at the rink back when we trained together and drove her home afterwards, I would always think of things I forgot to tell her, or new things would come to mind that I wanted to share with her. That just didn't happen with Grace.

I planted my feet on the floor when the doorbell echoed through my house, ready to get up to let Amy in, but Grace jumped up first.

"I'll get it," she insisted, and since it would have been silly to argue with her or race her to the door, I waited in the living room while Amy came inside and took off her coat and boots.

I could hear Grace pointing out the bathroom and kitchen before they came to join me, and annoyance shot through me that she would give Amy a tour of my house when I would have liked to do it myself, but I pushed that annoyance down. At least she was being nice to Amy, and as Amy herself had said, we didn't need tension between any of us.

"Sorry I'm late," Amy apologized again as she walked in, glancing around the space. My eyes followed her gaze, trying to imagine what it looked like to her. A typical bachelor pad in a lot of ways, the TV took up most of the wall, with none of the decorative flourishes my women friends had in their houses.

I could barely concentrate on the room, though, as my eyes drifted back to her. Having Amy in my house after all this time felt surreal. After four years apart, I'd honestly never imagined it would happen. I wanted so much more than simply having her there, but for that night, we would focus on business, as she requested. "It's no problem. What movie are we watching?"

Before Amy could answer, Grace came and sat next to me on the couch. Having expected she might, I'd chosen the middle seat, assuming I could then have Amy on my other side, but to my frustration, she took one of the other chairs in the room instead.

"Atonement. Have you seen it before?"

Amy scanned our faces for any sign of recognition but I didn't know it, and when I looked at Grace, she shook her head too.

"What's it about?" I asked.

"Well, it's a love story." Amy's eyes slid away from mine as she answered, as if looking at me while saying the word 'love' made her uncomfortable. "But a sad one. A young couple fall in love but get separated through a misunderstanding. I won't say too much more so you can see it for yourselves, but I think it has the potential for real drama on the ice."

With that rather vague introduction, the three of us settled in to watch the movie. Just over two hours later, tears streaked Grace's face, Amy wiped at her own cheeks, and I blinked fast to fight back the burning sting in my eyes. It didn't help that I could clearly see the parallels between what happened to the couple in the movie and the way that Amy and I had been separated by things we didn't completely understand.

Was that what she meant when she said she wanted us to be able to relate to the story?

"Sorry," Amy apologized as she got a look at our faces. "I know it's emotional, but that's kind of what I'm going for. The thrill and passion of their love, the pain of separation, the joy of reuniting, and the tragedy when you realize the actual ending."

"That's a lot for a four-minute program," I couldn't help pointing out, and Grace let out a half-sobbed laugh next to me in agreement, unable to speak.

"It is, but I think it could be amazing. Grace, you could have a beautiful green dress like the one Keira Knightley wears, and Austin, you could be in a soldier's uniform. I think it would look incredible."

I turned to Grace, who nodded thoughtfully. "I like it. I think it could work."

Amy beamed in delighted relief. "Austin? What do you think?"

"I trust you completely, so if you think this is the program for us, I'm all in."

Her smile somehow grew even brighter. "I guess we've got a program then. Now, we really need to get to work."

Chapter Two

~Amelia~

The next few weeks were so busy, I could hardly tell where one day ended and the next began. Austin's and Grace's costumes needed to be made and the music for their program cut. Brian and Austin both insisted that I go to Japan with them for the competition, to be there for their practices with the program still so new, so I had travel arrangements to make as well.

It had been a long time since I'd left the country, not since the Junior Worlds that Austin and I won back when we were skating together. It would be very strange to be backstage at a skating competition and not be competing, but I found myself looking forward to it just the same. On top of all of that, I tried to keep up with my schoolwork, my internship and my friends, but things were slipping, despite my best efforts.

Austin invited me to his place more than once, for dinner, for a movie, or just to hang out, but I literally didn't have time. I didn't even eat with my friends in the cafeteria anymore, resorting to munching on carrot sticks and granola bars while working on my assignments instead. Every spare second of my day got eaten up one way or another.

I reminded him that we had agreed to keep things professional anyway, and though I could tell my refusal disappointed him, he said that he understood.

A couple of days before we left for Japan, I was in the Urban Style office, finishing up some work for my internship, when I ran into Paul, the photographer who had helped me with my profile of Austin.

"I heard you're going overseas," he greeted me as we crossed paths in the office corridor. "NHK Trophy?"

"I... yes? How do you know that?"

He let out an easy, friendly laugh. "Your friend Gaby told me. We've been hanging out a little bit."

Gaby and Paul? She hadn't mentioned it, but then, I'd hardly had a chance to talk to her at all in the last few weeks. Were they 'hanging out' as friends or something more? I would have to remember to ask Gaby about it later and get the full scoop.

"She actually said NHK Trophy?" I asked, surprised that she would have known the name of the competition.

He chuckled again. "No, actually. I only knew that part because my brother will be there too. You'll have to say hi if you run into him."

I'd almost forgotten that Paul had a brother who used to skate. He told me that the day he gave me the photography lesson, the same day Austin and I finally cleared the air between us, and the conversation with Austin had overshadowed everything else. I literally hadn't thought of Paul's brother again since he mentioned him.

"Is he going to be there?"

"He'll be doing the backstage interviews," Paul explained before dropping a name that I knew very well indeed. "His name's Ben. Miller, obviously, like me."

My mouth literally dropped open, my jaw going slack in my surprise. *Ben Miller.* The same Ben who had almost kissed me all those years ago, the same night that Austin had kissed me for the one and only time. It had never once crossed my mind that he might be the brother Paul had mentioned, and why would it? Miller wasn't exactly a rare surname.

"Do you know him?" Paul asked, probably noticing my stunned expression.

"We skated at the same club in Ottawa for a little while. A long time ago."

"Really? Wow, small world, eh? I'll let him know you're coming, I'm sure he'd love to catch up. I've got to get to a meeting now, but have a great trip. Don't forget to take some pictures!"

Giving me a cheerful smile, he walked halfway down the hall before I managed to stutter out a thank you.

I hadn't seen Ben since the night of his party, the night before my accident. I hadn't seen any of the other skaters from the club in Ottawa since then. My mom and I left town almost immediately afterwards and I hadn't had a way of getting in touch with any of them since not only did my phone get destroyed in the accident but I hadn't had their numbers anyway.

From watching competitions on TV, I knew that Ben skated another two years after the last time I saw him before deciding to quit. He just couldn't seem to break through to the podium at the national level, and skating was an expensive sport to keep pursuing if you weren't getting the results you wanted.

It made me smile to hear he'd found a way to stay involved with the sport in some way, and it would be interesting to hear about how he landed his current job since I hoped to do exactly that kind of thing once I finished my journalism degree. Tracking him down in Japan, if I had any spare time, could be really interesting.

As soon as time crossed my mind, I glanced down at my watch and groaned. My next class would be starting in exactly the same amount of time it would take me to get there from the office, and as soon as it finished, I had to head back to the rink. Everything else would have to wait.

~Austin~

After my mom had been away from the rink for three weeks, I finally bit the bullet and went to visit her again.

"What have you been up to?" I asked as we sat down in the living room. Hopefully, she found herself a new hobby or maybe a new friend, anything to occupy some of her time during the forced break I put her on.

"I reviewed all the programs for all your main competitors this year," she started, and my stomach instantly sank. No such luck, apparently. "I made notes of some of the elements you might want to look at."

"That's not your job." Even in her semi-official capacity as my manager and publicist, she wouldn't be expected to do things like that. "And you know I don't watch the other teams. I can't do anything about their programs, so there's no point wasting my time or yours looking at them."

Her lips pursed into a frown. "Well, I need to be useful somehow. You banned me from the rink, you won't answer my calls, so what am I supposed to do?"

"Nobody banned you," I corrected her, doing my best to keep my tone even and not take the bait she dangled in front of me. "I just asked you to take a break. You have, and I appreciate it, but I think it's time that we talk about this, Mom. This can't be your whole life. What are you going to do when I stop skating?"

Her eyes widened as if the thought had never occurred to her. "Well, that's not going to happen anytime soon, so we have plenty of time..."

"It may be sooner than you think." I cut her off before taking a deep breath, debating just how much I wanted to share with her. My plans for the future had been coming together in the back of my mind for a while, and with Amy reappearing in my life, they'd gotten more defined. "Depending on how this season goes, it might be my last one."

As I would have predicted, shock and dismay coloured my mom's expression. "What are you talking about? You're only 23, you have at least one more Olympic cycle in top condition, maybe two..."

"To do what?" I interrupted. "We won the silver at World's last year. If we can get an Olympic medal, what more do we need to prove?"

"But you love it," she insisted.

"I do, but it's the skating I love, not the competition. All the things I love about it, I can keep doing after retiring."

"Is this about your foundation?" Her nose wrinkled as if 'foundation' were some kind of dirty word.

"Maybe. I don't know for sure yet, but what I'm trying to say is that I'm going to move on eventually, so you need to start thinking about what you're going to do with the rest of your life too."

She kept asking questions as if I hadn't spoken. "Have you told Grace about all this?"

My stomach twisted at the thought of Grace finding out about any of this from my mom. "No, and please don't say anything to her just yet. We'll have this conversation when we're both ready for it."

"Is this because of Amy?"

She couldn't hide the sneer in her voice that always accompanied Amy's name, and my jaw clenched as I took another deep inhale before responding.

"You don't get to ask me about Amy or talk to me about her at all. Do you understand that? You ruined our partnership on purpose. You've more than had your revenge for whatever slight you think she ever did to you. From now on, you stay away from her entirely."

My words had the expected effect on my mother, being none at all. She eyed me as coolly and unapologetically as always. "You're never this protective of Grace."

"Because you never tried to ruin Grace's life!" I exploded, my patience at an end. "I mean it, Mom. If you can't put aside this petty grudge you've always had against Amy, then you're not welcome back at the rink. You aren't invited to Japan, or the Olympics, or anything. It's up to you. If you can behave like a decent human being and leave all of this childishness behind, then fine, you can finish the season as my manager. But if not, we're done right now. Am I clear?"

Defiance flared in my mom's eyes, but she held her tongue, recognizing the sincerity in my voice. I could almost see her debating with herself, trying to figure out how far she could push things and what would be worth it for her.

Finally, she grimaced. "Fine. I won't talk to her or say anything about her, if that's what you want."

"It is. If you can stick to that, you're welcome to come back to the rink tomorrow, but if I hear that you step out of line with her even once, I'm pulling the plug."

"I understand," she replied stiffly. "You know I just want what's best for you."

A sarcastic snort slipped through before I could stop it. "I know that's what you think, but you don't actually have the first idea of what's really best for me. From now on, I'm going to be the one making those decisions."

After getting her grudging agreement, I drove back home, reviewing the conversation in my head. I had been as clear as I possibly could have been. Her whole life had revolved around my skating for so long that I didn't want to cut her out of my last season entirely. As long as she could rein herself in and stay away from Amy like she promised, I could deal with her being around.

Now, I just had to hope that she actually meant what she said and that I wouldn't regret giving her another chance.

FIGURING IT OUT

~Amelia~

The zipper of my suitcase strained dangerously as I tried to shove just one more piece of clothing inside. I had just leaned over onto it to try to force it closed when my phone rang in my pocket, making me jump and, before I knew it, the top of the suitcase sprang back open again. With a groan, I reached into my pocket and grabbed my phone, excitement quickly replacing my frustration as Austin's name flashed across the screen.

"Hey," I answered, trying to sound calm and collected rather than flustered. "Are you here?"

The day before, he offered to drive me to the airport for the flight to Japan. He said he wanted to save me the cab fare, but I suspected he was afraid that if he didn't, I would show up late and miss the flight entirely. Given how insanely busy I'd been, it wouldn't be impossible.

"I'm parked right outside," he confirmed. "Are you ready? Do you need me to come give you a hand?"

"I'm trying to get my suitcase closed. It might be a little too full."

His laugh sounded warm and comforting in my ear. "I've got room in mine. Just throw some stuff in a bag and you can toss it in. Like always."

The warmth from his voice spread to my chest with those last two words. Efficient packing had never been a particular skill of mine, so when we used to travel to competitions together, he always left half his suitcase empty so that I could toss whatever didn't fit in my bag into his.

It made me happier than it should have that he still remembered that.

I'd been so focused on the program and everything else that I needed to get done before we left that I'd barely had a second to actually get excited about the trip itself. That little reminder of what it had been like to travel with Austin, to go somewhere new with him and spend time together off the ice, suddenly made me realize just how much I was looking forward to this. For the next five days, I didn't have to be a university student and magazine intern. My whole world would revolve around skating, locked into a little bubble of our own making, and it sounded kind of wonderful.

"I'll be down in two minutes," I promised into the phone. Hanging up, I grabbed a handful of clothes out of my suitcase at random, threw them into a canvas bag, pulled the zipper closed on the now slightly-less-stuffed suitcase, and headed out the door.

Austin stood outside his car in front of the dorm, as he said, and my stomach fluttered at the sight of him. That response to him had always been outside of my control, and I suspected it always would be. No matter what I tried to tell myself, my body knew the truth.

He opened the passenger door for me as I walked up, just like he always used to, and grabbed the bags from my hand. As I got myself settled, he tossed everything in the trunk and came around to the driver's side.

"Are you ready for your life to change?" he asked as he sat down next to me, giving me a warm smile.

He meant the change that would come with debuting my program on an international stage. I knew that, but all I could think about was how we said we would keep things professional until this trip. Now that the trip had arrived, I realized just how vague those words had been. Did that agreement expire once we got on the plane? When we landed? When the competition ended, or not until after we got home?

I didn't want to complicate anything or throw him off his game when he needed to concentrate, but when he gave me that smile, I felt sixteen again, wanting nothing more than to have his attention focused on me.

With a great deal of effort, I forced myself to stick to the topic of skating, the reason we were there. "I can't wait for you and Grace to win with your new program."

"We've definitely got a much better chance with this program than we did with the last one," he said, his eyes on the road as he pulled out into the street, still with a smile on his face. "Maybe if we win, we can go celebrate with some actual Japanese food. Not burger sushi like last time."

A laugh bubbled its way past my lips. "I haven't thought about that in a long time."

Austin and I competed in a Junior Grand Prix competition in Nagano five years earlier, and Austin's mom had been so insistent about not eating sushi that she dragged us to an American diner-style restaurant when Austin and I would have much rather tried some of the local food. He cut up his burger and rolled pieces of meat in the bun to look like sushi, just to annoy her.

"I thought your mom's head might explode when you pulled the chopsticks out of your bag to eat it!" I reminded him as the memory came back to me. I laughed so hard that I snorted, making him laugh too, and my hands shot up to cover my face as my cheeks burned. "I can't seem to stop doing that."

"You shouldn't ever stop. It's the best way for me to tell when you find something really funny. I like it."

My cheeks still red, I lowered my hands and looked out the window of the car, watching the city go by. I didn't know what made me blush more: my snort or the fact that he said he liked it. "That was a fun trip."

"They were all fun with you, Amy."

My eyes returned to him, wondering if he was still joking around, but his smile had melted into something far more wistful, and I quickly looked away again as my heart rate picked up speed.

Back then, I never thought he enjoyed our time together in the same way I did, but now that he'd admitted to me that he'd had feelings for me too, maybe I'd had it wrong. Maybe I had to reevaluate a lot of things I thought I knew.

Every trip with him had been memorable, but I had a feeling the trip ahead of us would surpass them all, in ways I couldn't even begin to imagine yet.

~Austin~

The time alone with Amy in the car was the first real time we'd had alone together in weeks. She claimed her inability to spend time with me had nothing to do with me personally, and I knew she was busy. She'd warned me she would be. However, now that we had the new program ready to go, I wanted to move on with our relationship, and I wanted this trip to be the start.

For the next few days, the only obligations either of us had were on the ice. The rest of the time would belong to us, and I intended to make the most of it.

At the airport, we headed for the check-in area where the rest of our travelling group were already waiting. Grace had brought her parents, my mom was coming, and our coach Brian and his husband Kevin rounded out the group, along with Amy and me. Brian had booked all the tickets, and I hoped there would be some flexibility in the seat assignments. With a thirteen-hour flight ahead of us, I wanted to spend that time with Amy.

As usual, we'd all arrived early in case there were any issues at security with taking our skates through. Checking our skates was never an option. If the skates didn't arrive with us, we didn't compete, simple as that, so we couldn't let them out of our sight.

Once we were through security and at the gate, everyone spread out on the benches and I grabbed the seat next to Amy. "What seat are you in on the plane?"

"I'm not sure. Let me check." She pulled out the boarding pass that she'd been handed earlier and squinted down at it from behind her glasses. "39C, it looks like."

Damn it. Mine was in row 42, so I'd need to ask around and see who I could trade with so we ended up sitting together.

"Can I see it for a second?" She held out the boarding pass to me and I snatched it from her hand, walking away without a word.

"Austin..." she started to protest from behind me, but I didn't wait to give her a chance to complain or to tell me I should sit with anyone else. She was so worried about causing problems for me, she couldn't see that the only thing I considered a problem was not being with her.

I started with Brian, figuring he would be easiest. He and Kevin had taken seats close to the gate where they could keep an eye on things. "Which seats are you guys in?"

"40A and C," Kevin answered, not even needing to look at their passes. "And no, we're not trading with you."

"I didn't even say anything," I said, but he just shook his head at me.

"Thirteen-hour flight, Austin. I'm sitting with my husband."

Obviously, I wouldn't be getting anywhere with them, so I tried my mom next. "Where are you sitting, Mom?"

"41C. I think I'm with Grace's mom."

They got along well enough, their relationship having been mended when Grace and I started skating together again, so I would leave well enough alone there, although I did wonder why Grace's parents weren't sitting together. I glanced around for Grace's dad, but he'd disappeared, probably to pick up some food. Grace herself stood with her mom near the gate, so I walked over to them, hoping for the best. If she and Amy were sitting together, she'd probably be happy to trade. The only way I could see it being a problem would be if she had...

"42A." Just like Kevin, she didn't need to check her pass. She did, however, peer down curiously at mine that I held in my hand, and her smile brightened as she glanced back up. "Oh, I'm next to you! That's perfect. We can figure out what we want to do with our off time in Tokyo. We haven't had a chance to talk about it yet but I've got a few ideas already."

Despite the disappointment clenching my stomach, I plastered on a smile. How could I tell her that I'd rather sit with Amy than with her? There wasn't any nice way to say it, no matter how true it was, and knocking her confidence going into the competition would be a bad idea all around.

"I guess I'll see you on the plane, then."

Cursing my luck, I headed back towards Amy, but my steps slowed as I got closer to where I'd left her. Next to her, a man around my age had taken my seat, talking and laughing with her. He looked vaguely familiar, but I couldn't place him.

"Hey," I said as I got back over to them, focusing my attention solely on Amy. "Here's your boarding pass."

"Thanks." She sounded confused and perhaps even a bit disappointed as she glanced down at it and realized nothing had changed. Maybe she'd been secretly hoping to sit with me too.

The man next to her leaned over, peering at the slip of paper in her hand. "39C? No way. You're right next to me. I'm 39A."

Amy smiled at him, their faces way too close together for my liking. "Really? Wow, what are the odds?"

What were the odds, indeed? Who the hell *was* this guy?

Amy must have noticed my confusion because she nodded over at me, still addressing the other man. "You remember Austin, right?"

"Of course." His smile turned a little cooler as his eyes moved to me. "Nice to see you again."

When I didn't reply, since I still didn't know what was going on, Amy jumped in again. "And you remember Ben, Austin? He used to skate with us in Ottawa. He's going to Japan too."

Ben. My mind flashed back to the house party four years earlier and the arrogant new guy at the club giving a 16-year-old Amy a drink and taking her up to his bedroom. *That* Ben? No wonder I didn't recognize him. I'd done my best to block his existence from my memory entirely.

What the hell was he doing there? Why was he going to Japan? And how the hell could I relax, knowing he would be sitting next to Amy for the whole flight?

This was going to be the longest flight of my entire life.

~**Amelia**~

When Austin stole my boarding pass, hope sparked inside me that he had a plan to get us to sit together on the flight. With nowhere else to go and minimal interruptions, it would have given us a chance to really talk to each other in a way we hadn't been able to do with all the other noise of our lives at the moment.

However, when he returned, he handed my pass back to me without another word, and it turned out Ben would be sitting next to me instead.

He spotted me before I saw him. I'd been busy sending Gaby a last-minute text before boarding when I heard someone say my name. Not Mia, the name everyone other than Austin called me, but my old name.

"Amy?"

Glancing up, it only took a couple of seconds for me to recognize the man standing in front of me. "Ben?"

"Hi."

His wide grin looked just as kind and inviting as I remembered it. He'd matured over the past four years, like we all had, and a trim beard lined his jaw. His eyes gave him away, though; his eyes and his smile. I could see traces of both the man I briefly knew in Ottawa and of his brother, who I'd been working with for the past few months.

He brought Paul up as he sat down next to me in the seat I'd been saving for Austin. "My brother mentioned that he worked with someone who'd skated with me before, and that you'd be in Japan. When he sent me the picture he took of you skating with Austin, I couldn't believe it."

"You recognized me? Even though Paul gave you my new name?"

"Of course. Your hair's different." He reached out to brush the dark strands back from my face. "And these are new." He tapped on my glasses playfully. "But your form on the ice in those photos? It couldn't have been anyone else."

That seemed ironic, since Austin hadn't noticed the similarities. To be fair, though, he'd been skating with me rather than watching me. Maybe he'd have noticed it more from a distance.

Once Austin joined us and I reintroduced them, the three of us chatted until the airline staff announced boarding for the flight. The conversation centered on the upcoming competition: Austin asked what Ben would be doing there and Ben told us a bit about his job with the TV network. He would almost certainly be interviewing Austin and Grace after they skated, so we all would have run into each other eventually even if we hadn't met at the airport.

Austin seemed a bit tense as we talked, which I put down to pre-flight nerves. Although he loved going to new places, he didn't particularly like the travelling part of it. He wasn't a nervous flier, exactly, he just didn't enjoy it, and this would be a particularly long flight. I hadn't been looking forward to it either, but at least I had Ben to keep me company. I'd been worried I would end up with Mrs Black, which would have been an absolute nightmare.

Since she returned to the rink, she hadn't said a word to me, good or bad, and I'd prefer to keep it that way. I could only assume that Austin said something to her to keep her away from me but I hadn't had a chance to ask him about it yet.

When the time came to board, Austin turned to Ben.

"If you'd like, we could switch seats for part of the flight. It would give you a chance to get to know Grace a bit."

He would be sitting with Grace, then, apparently. I did my best to ignore the stab of unreasonable jealousy digging into my stomach.

Ben politely declined. "I appreciate the offer, but I actually try not to socialize too much with skaters I'm covering. It's better if I can remain impartial."

Austin threw me a look that I couldn't interpret before heading further down the aisle to take his seat while Ben and I settled down in our own row.

He wasted no time before diving into conversation. "I heard about your accident, obviously. All of us at the club did." His eyes held plenty of sympathy but no pity as he swiftly moved on. "What have you been up to since then?"

We talked about my schoolwork and about his job, and as I hoped, he had plenty of useful tips on how to get into reporting on skating if that's what I wanted to do.

My choreography work piqued his interest the most, though. "Maybe it's the reporter in me talking, but it's a great story: coming back from your injury and finding a new niche for yourself, rising above adversity and all of that. And working with your old partner? The public would eat it up."

"Well, I don't think anyone will make that connection. I'm being credited as Mia Wilson, not Amy Gardiner, so people won't even know that it's me. I don't intend to make any of it public."

"I'm not sure how realistic that is, Mia." In the short time we'd spent together, he already remembered to call me Mia, unlike Austin who didn't even try. "If the program is as good as it's bound to be, people are going to be curious about you. They'll want to know your background, and if everyone you're travelling with knows who you are, someone is bound to let something slip. Personally, I think it would be better to be upfront about it and get ahead of the story, spin it to your advantage."

He might have had a point about that. It didn't work out to try to keep my identity hidden from Austin, and I remembered how relieved I felt when I finally confessed the truth to the magazine's editor.

Maybe Ben was right.

Even so, the idea of making my past known to the world at large still didn't appeal to me. "I don't want people feeling sorry for me. That was the whole reason I changed my name in the first place. The pity is really frustrating."

"Trust me, when people get a look at your program, no one is going to be feeling sorry for you."

The flattering words made me blush. "You haven't even seen it yet."

"No, but I saw the one you created for you and Austin, all those years ago. I saw you guys working on it at the rink and it blew me away, so I can imagine how good your new one is too."

Just like on that night at his housewarming party, I was touched by how much attention he seemed to pay to me, attention I'd been completely unaware of.

We talked for a while longer until I realized nearly everyone around us had gone to sleep or wanted to. I excused myself to go use the bathroom before I tried to get some rest myself. The bathroom at the back of the plane was closer than the one in the middle, so I headed that way.

"Amy."

Austin's voice was hardly above a whisper, but it still made me jump as I walked down the aisle. It took me a second to find him, and when I did, my stomach knotted. He sat in a window seat, his phone in his hand, and next to him, asleep and curled up against him with her head on his shoulder, was Grace.

To any casual observer, they looked exactly like the off-ice couple everyone thought they were.

"Hey," I answered, trying not to let my jealousy show. Did they always pretend to be a couple when they travelled? Did he choose to sit next to her instead of me?

"Everything okay?" he whispered, obviously trying not to wake Grace. His consideration was sweet, but it made my stomach ache even more. It had started to seem like my hopes for this trip were a little unrealistic. How could we start something when his life remained so firmly tied to hers for the next few months?

I nodded, forcing a smile. "Just going to the bathroom, then I'm going to try to sleep. You're not tired?"

"Can't turn my brain off," he explained, shrugging his one free shoulder. "Too excited about this trip, I guess."

Did he mean the competition, or was he talking about us? I still didn't know what he had in mind for us this weekend, or if he wanted to wait until we got home before we took the next step, whatever that might be.

"Well, try to rest," I advised. "You've got training tomorrow."

"I know, coach. Thanks for looking out for me."

His teasing tone made me smile, but before I could say anything else, someone came up from behind me, also heading for the bathroom, so I had to keep moving. I bade him goodnight and kept walking down the aisle.

~Austin~

A deep sigh of frustration deflated my shoulders as Amy walked away.

I hadn't missed the look on her face when she saw Grace asleep on me. The look only lasted a second but I could guess what she must be feeling.

Being Grace's pillow certainly hadn't been my idea and I had just been thinking about how nice it would have been if Amy had been the one sitting next to me, if it had been her resting against me instead, when she suddenly appeared as if I'd conjured her from my thoughts.

Why didn't I just move Grace before Amy saw us? I had thought about trying to prop her up somewhere else, but I didn't want to wake her. She had trouble sleeping on planes and since I wanted her to be as well rested as possible, I decided to just let her sleep. Having seen Amy's reaction, I regretted that choice more than ever.

Eventually, I managed to get some sleep too, and after what felt like days rather than hours, we finally landed in Tokyo. As I helped Grace to pack up all her things from around our seats, I found her boarding pass shoved down the back of the seat pocket. She quickly snatched it from me, but not before I got a glimpse of the seat assignment.

41C.

Not 42A, the seat she'd claimed as hers. 41C was the row ahead, where my mom sat next to hers.

"Did you and my mom switch seats?" I asked as she shoved the boarding pass away and pulled out her phone instead.

"Hmm?" She acted as though she hadn't heard me while she logged onto the Wi-Fi.

"Grace." I took a deep breath, trying to temper my annoyance. Had she done this on purpose? Had my mom? "You told me this was your seat."

"Your mom wanted to sit with my mom," she explained, still not looking at me. "We switched before you asked me where I was sitting. It worked out best for all of us."

Seriously? I just sat through thirteen hours of tedium for no good reason? My jaw clenched to keep me from saying anything I might regret.

"Hey, look at this," Grace said, holding up her phone and obviously trying to change the subject. "Someone just posted this, they must have been sitting nearby. Isn't it cute?"

My stomach twisted even further as I saw the photo she'd found on Instagram: a picture of Grace asleep on my shoulder. I hadn't noticed anyone taking a picture of us, but in the photo, I was looking down at my own phone, so I must have been distracted.

At least, *I* knew I was looking at my phone, but from the angle of the photo, it almost looked like I was looking down at Grace and clearly, people were choosing to see it that way. There were already several comments about how sweet we were together, what a great couple we were, all the usual nonsense that went along with our refusal to deny the rumours about us.

Amy hadn't really had to deal with that side of things yet since she'd only been with us at the rink where all our training mates knew that we weren't really together, but now, I realized that she was going to have to watch all weekend as Grace and I did our usual dance of looking like we *could* be involved without ever saying for sure one way or the other.

This whole trip suddenly seemed a lot more complicated than I wanted it to be.

Chapter Three

~Amelia~

The first day in Japan sped by in a flurry of activity. Austin and Grace had two practice sessions that day after we landed, one in the late morning and one later in the afternoon. In the morning they worked mostly on their rhythm dance while the afternoon focused on the free dance. Since I couldn't go on the ice with them in the official practice sessions, I stood at the boards instead, calling out suggestions for improvements or things to watch. The free dance wasn't perfect yet, but considering they'd only really been training it for three weeks, I felt good about it. Even better, *they* felt good about it.

When they skated the whole program through, I recorded it to review later, and I didn't miss many of the other coaches at the boards with me watching Austin and Grace closely and whispering amongst themselves.

They were taking notice, and that seemed like a good sign.

When the afternoon session finished, Austin exited the locker room before Grace, heading towards me with purpose. His damp hair clung to his forehead and the smell of his cologne hit me all over again as he approached. Although he always looked good, his straight-off-the-ice look had to be one of my favourites.

"Do you have any plans this evening?"

I planned to review the video I took, looking for improvements we could make, but that wouldn't take all night. "Not really. Brian said he and Kevin are having dinner at the hotel and I could join them if I wanted to."

"Tell them you're busy. I want to take you somewhere."

His firm tone made my heart speed up, though I did my best not to let it show. "You need to get your rest for tomorrow."

"I know. It won't be a late night, I promise."

"Where are we..." I started to ask, but Austin cut me off as Grace approached, changing the subject before she got into earshot.

"The exit from the step sequence felt a lot smoother today," he said, as if we'd been talking about their program all along, obviously not wanting her to know what we'd *actually* been talking about. He turned to Grace as she fell into place beside him. "What do you think?"

The way she glanced back and forth between us suggested she didn't completely buy Austin's cover-up, but she answered his question anyway. "It felt okay, I guess. I'm too hungry to think straight right now. Let's go back to the hotel and get supper."

She tried to link her arm through his, but Austin stepped away. "Actually, I'm going to have an early night. I'll just get some room service, but I know Brian and Kevin are going to the hotel restaurant. You and your parents could join them if you want."

A knot of discomfort formed in my chest as he lied about his plans. Why wouldn't he just tell Grace the truth?

She was obviously disappointed in his response, though not for the same reason I was. "We always have supper together after practice."

He gave her a tight smile, nothing like his usual easy grin, but she didn't seem to notice the difference. "I know, but I'm still tired from the flight. I didn't sleep well."

Brian joined us, ending the discussion, and we all returned to the hotel together. Austin didn't say anything else to me about going out before he and Grace both went into their own rooms, so I went into mine too, still not sure about where we'd left things. However, just a few minutes later, someone knocked quietly on my door. When I opened it, Austin stood on the other side, his dimple on display as he grinned down at me with his real smile.

"Are you ready to finally go on a date with me?"

That answered one question, at least. Apparently, he thought the time limit on our professional-only relationship had run out now that we were in Japan, and the confirmation immediately made the butterflies in my stomach take flight.

However, there were still a few other things I wanted to clear up before I let either of us get carried away.

~Austin~

Amy fidgeted with the hem of her jacket as we walked down the hall to the elevators, and as soon as we were inside, she turned to me. "Why are you lying to Grace? Why not just tell her that we're doing something together?"

The word 'lying' made me grimace, but I couldn't deny I had. I could only do my best to explain. "Grace and I have a more complicated partnership than you and I did. She's sensitive about a lot of things and it throws her off her game if she gets too worried. I don't want her stressing about you and me while we're competing."

Amy's sigh hinted at her disappointment in that answer even before she said the words. "I would think that you, of all people, wouldn't want there to be any kind of secrets in your partnership."

That stung, as the thought of everything that had gone wrong between us always would, and I knew she had a point. "Like I said, it's complicated, but maybe you could talk through it with me and help me decide how to handle it? To be honest, I would love to have someone I could really talk to. I tried to get advice from some of the other guys at the club, but they just think it's funny that she wants more and I don't. I don't have a lot of other friends and it's not really the kind of thing I can talk to my mom about."

Amy's shudder at that idea made me laugh, and she finally cracked a smile too. By the time we reached the lobby, the mood had lightened and we both turned our focus to the night ahead as I led her out of the hotel and onto the street.

"Where are we going?" she asked. Our strides were perfectly matched, just like they'd always been on the ice.

"For sushi." My conspiratorial wink was meant to remind her of both our earlier conversation and our last trip to Japan. "Better late than never."

We took the subway to Shinjuku where the neon lights lit up the street so brightly it almost looked like daytime. Walking side by side, we wandered the streets for a while, pointing out fun things in the stores or at the street vendors.

Before long, a few Japanese skating fans recognized me. Amy noticed them before I did.

"Don't look now but you're about to be swarmed," she teased.

Thankfully, that was an exaggeration. They politely asked for a photo, and after I'd posed with them, they all thanked me profusely.

"Where's Grace?" one of them asked, looking around as though she might be hiding just out of sight.

"She's resting at the hotel to make sure we skate our best this weekend."

They wished me luck and went on their way, never sparing a glance for the woman at my side who hung back, not wanting to intrude. Would it ever get less frustrating that the best skater I'd ever worked with never got the recognition she deserved?

Eventually, we settled into a small restaurant that I'd heard good things about. Sitting across the table from her, it hardly seemed possible that we were there. She'd been back in my life for weeks, but sometimes, it still felt like I might blink and she would disappear again.

"Have you travelled much since…"

My question trailed off as I realized I didn't know exactly what to say. Since we stopped skating together? Since I accidentally abandoned her? Since her life completely changed?

Luckily, she didn't make me finish. "No. Toronto and St John's are pretty much the only places I've been."

A pang of grief shot through my chest as I thought of all the places I'd been with Grace and how it could have been Amy with me all that time. Would that feeling of loss ever get easier?

Looking for a distraction from thoughts of the past, I turned my attention to the menu. Soon, we were both laughing as we tried to decipher what everything was and what we wanted. We managed to order and both sat back with our drinks, falling into a comfortable silence for a moment before Amy broke it.

"You were going to tell me about Grace and why you're lying to her."

I really disliked that word, but I didn't argue with her use of it. Instead, I explained to her as honestly as I could about how Grace seemed to want more out of our relationship than I did, and how I'd tried to tell her I wasn't interested without hurting her feelings.

"This ridiculous game that we have to play, pretending to be together for the media, really doesn't help anything. I feel like sometimes she plays into it more than necessary, but I can't really call her out on it without it sounding like an accusation, which would send her right into a downward spiral."

To prove my point, I pulled out my phone and pulled up Grace's Instagram feed. Half the photos on it were pictures of me or pictures of the two of us together. We were a team, sure, but we barely ever saw each other outside the rink. Looking at her profile, no one would ever guess that.

Amy's wince grew strong the further she scrolled. "Okay, I see it. I didn't realize it was this bad. You're sure you're not leading her on at all?"

"I really don't see how I could be. You didn't think I liked you even when I did, so I'm pretty sure I'm not giving the green light to someone I'm definitely not interested in."

Amy's cheeks flushed pink as she looked down at the chopsticks on the table, playing with them with her fingers. "And you're not even a little bit interested? She's very pretty."

Whether that question came from what she'd seen between me and Grace on the plane, something Grace might have said or done, or simply any lingering doubts she had about my feelings back when we were skating together, I couldn't be sure, but at least I could set her mind completely at rest on this point.

"I'm not even a little bit interested in Grace. If you ever see anything that makes it look otherwise, it's not true. I know I've broken my promise to you before, and I'm lying to Grace now, so I understand that it might be hard to take my words at face value, but I need you to trust me on this, Amy. There's nothing between me and Grace. The only person I'm interested in right now is you."

That sweet, happy smile of hers spread across her face, making my chest fill with warmth, but all too soon, she pulled it back. "I do trust you, but it's not quite that easy, is it? Not when everyone thinks you're dating someone else."

"I don't care about everyone else. It's my life, so what Grace or my mom or the judges or anyone else wants doesn't matter. If you agree to go out with me, I'll go out on the street right now and tell everyone that you're my girlfriend."

Part of me hoped that she *would* agree right then and there, but Amy just shook her head, a smile playing on her lips.

"You were just saying how sensitive Grace is, and the last thing you want to do is mess things up on the ice right now. Don't you think you should at least talk to her about it first before you make any grand announcement?"

Although neither of us were being completely serious, the fact of the matter was it would crush Grace if word got out about me and Amy before I told her myself. As much as I didn't want to date her, I also didn't want to hurt her unnecessarily.

"Let's make a plan, then." Amy had always liked to plan things out in advance, so this should appeal to her. "As soon as the competition is over, I'll talk to Grace and tell her that you and I are seeing each other and we're not going to hide it. That'll give her a month to get over it before the Grand Prix final when we have to compete in public again. Until then, we'll keep things low-key and 'professional', just like we have been."

Three more days of hiding how I felt. It sounded like a hell of a long time, but at least having an end in sight would make it a little more bearable. I'd already waited almost five years. What was three more days in the grand scheme of things?

Amy took a breath, thinking it over, and I held my own breath waiting for her response.

When she smiled up at me, the whole world seemed brighter. "That sounds reasonable. When the competition is over and you talk to her, we'll talk about what comes next."

"What comes next is that I'm taking you on a proper date before we go home. Save the night after the free dance for me. We'll call tonight a practice run. If I don't get to kiss you at the end of it, it doesn't count."

Although she laughed, I didn't miss the way her cheeks reddened when I mentioned kissing, and I felt that blush all the way through my body.

Luckily, our food arrived before I could get too carried away with my thoughts, and we spent the rest of the evening talking and teasing one another and simply enjoying each other's company. It felt just as easy and natural as I always thought it would.

If that was a preview of what it would be like to date her, the next three days couldn't go quickly enough.

Chapter Four

~Amelia~

The next morning, I stood rinkside at the main arena, watching Austin and Grace run through their free dance again, so focused on the ice that the gentle tap on my shoulder nearly made me jump out of my skin.

"Whoa, sorry," Ben apologized, holding his hands up in surrender as I pressed my hand to my chest, trying to catch my breath and slow my heart back down to a reasonable speed. "I didn't realize you were that far in the zone."

"My fault," I managed to gasp. "I didn't see you there."

"Apparently," he agreed with a grin before gesturing with his head to the ice. "They look good out there. They shouldn't have any problem with this field."

I hoped not. Austin and Grace's main competitors, the French team that had won Worlds the year before as well as Skate America earlier in the season, weren't in attendance. The highest-ranked team at this competition had come fourth at last year's Worlds. If Austin and Grace didn't win, it would be a cause for concern, but being the favourites brought its own kind of pressures and they couldn't afford to be overconfident.

"I should have been a dancer," Ben said, still watching the ice. "My footwork was always the best part of my programs. I just couldn't jump to save my life."

He was being pretty hard on himself. "Your Axel gave you trouble but your triple Lutz was beautiful."

"And I never got my quad consistent," he countered. "But I'm flattered you remember."

He turned to me with a smile as he said it and I could feel a blush creeping up my cheeks. Somehow, being there with him and him looking at me like that took me back to the night he almost kissed the shy, sixteen-year-old version of me in his bedroom.

Not that I wanted Ben to kiss me anymore. I didn't, not when the guy of my dreams had finally told me that he wanted me to be his girlfriend. I hadn't been able to think of anything else all night as I tossed and turned in my bed, unable to sleep.

All we had to do was get through the next three days and we could finally be together just like I'd always wanted. I had to pinch myself every time I thought about it.

I didn't feel anything like that for Ben, but being around him reminded me that a relationship *could* be simple and straightforward. You liked someone, you told them so, and that was it. It sounded like heaven.

If only things could have been that easy with Austin.

"Why didn't you dance, then?" I asked him, trying to refocus my thoughts back to skating and our conversation.

"There weren't any girls in my club I wanted to dance with," he replied, still giving me that slightly teasing smile. "I must have just been at the wrong club."

"Amy?"

Austin's voice came from a lot closer than I expected, and I turned back to the ice to see him and Grace both standing a short distance away, a frown marring his handsome face as he looked between me and Ben.

"Can we work on that transition now?"

"Of course," I quickly agreed, feeling guilty that I'd lost track of what they were doing. After reviewing the video from the day before, I'd told Austin and Grace that I wanted to make a change to the transition into one of their spins. It would look smoother without affecting the difficulty level.

"I'll let you get back to it," Ben said, flashing Austin and Grace a smile before turning his grin back on me. "Come by the broadcast booth later and say hi. I'll give you a tour if you like."

He wandered off and I turned my full attention back to the ice. Austin picked up on what I wanted right away but it took a few attempts before Grace had the positioning right. They did the full run-through of their dance incorporating the new transition, and as I'd hoped, it looked much cleaner.

With their practice finished, Austin and Grace had a couple of media appearances before they headed back to the hotel to rest before their final practice session later that afternoon. It would have only raised questions if I tagged along, and since I had nothing else to do, I decided to take Ben up on his offer of a tour.

It didn't take long to find the spot in the stands with his network's logo, and I found him at the desk there, sitting with a man and woman whom I recognized from watching skating coverage on TV. I nearly backed away when I saw them, not wanting to interrupt, but Ben caught my eye and gestured for me to come over.

"Hey, Mia, glad you could make it. Jennifer, Rob, I'm going to head out unless you need me for anything right now?"

They assured him they didn't and went back to whatever preparations they were making for the broadcast. As promised, Ben showed me around the booth, giving me tons of little tips and insights into what went into the behind-the-scenes preparation for a broadcast like this, before asking what my plans were for the rest of the day.

"Not much. It's my first time at one of these events where I'm not skating, so I'm not quite sure what to do with myself in the downtime. It seems like such a waste to sit around waiting for the next practice."

"That is absolutely a waste and I won't allow it."

His wink made my cheeks colour again, no matter how I tried to fight it. Everything he said felt flirty, but maybe that was just the way he talked. It didn't have to be anything special for me. Should I tell him I was sort of seeing someone? How could I explain the situation between Austin and me when I only barely understood it myself?

Before I could decide whether or not to bring it up, Ben continued. "I'm going to do a bit of sightseeing, maybe go visit some of the temples or shrines. You're welcome to come with me if you want."

"It sounds better than sitting alone in my hotel room," I admitted.

"That's the kind of enthusiasm I was going for."

We both laughed, and before long, I was glad I'd agreed. The next few hours were a lot of fun. Ben was good company, really funny and easy to talk to. Now that I knew he and Paul were brothers, I could definitely see some common family traits.

He told me some fun stories about Paul growing up and we talked about my classes at university. Although we never said we wouldn't talk about skating or about Austin and Grace, it felt like we'd both subconsciously agreed to avoid those topics and we still had plenty of things to talk about.

He certainly didn't try to make any kind of romantic move, and I felt completely comfortable with him by the time he said he needed to head back to the arena.

Fishing my phone out of my pocket, I gasped as I got a look at the time and saw the missed messages from Austin.

> What are you doing for lunch?

> Do you want to come hang out before we go back to the rink?

> Where are you?

I must have left my phone on silent and didn't feel it buzzing through the thick lining of my coat. I sent off a quick reply.

> Sorry, I forgot to turn my sound back up. I'm on my way to the arena now, I'll meet you there.

When I arrived, Austin and Grace were already in the locker rooms getting ready so I took my spot by the boards as the previous group finished their practice, watching the couples curiously. The sound of giggling from behind me caught my attention, and I turned around to see a group of girls sitting in the front row, looking straight at me and whispering amongst themselves.

That's weird.

I glanced around, wondering if there was someone close to me they might be looking at instead of me, but no one else was nearby. Feeling a little self-conscious, I turned back to the ice, wishing I'd taken a minute to check myself in the mirror before coming out there. Was there something wrong with the way I looked? My paranoia grew until finally, the skaters left the ice and the next group came out, including Austin and Grace.

Brian took his spot further down the boards, where he liked to stand, while I stayed put. This session, they would mostly be working on their rhythm dance, the one they'd be skating the next day, and I didn't have much to do on that one. I probably didn't need to be there at all, but I wanted to stay close at hand in case they needed me.

Before they'd even finished warming up, another person slid into place next to me, one who hadn't spoken to me directly since my true identity came to light. I didn't even have to look right at her to see who it was; her stiff, unyielding profile seen from the corner of my eye told me all I needed to know.

"It didn't take you long to start causing trouble," Mrs Black said.

I blinked over at her in surprise, both from the fact that she'd approached me at all and even more so because of her words. "What are you talking about?"

"That innocent act has never worked with me," she sneered at me. "And it certainly won't work now. I know what you're trying to do."

That came as news to me, because as far as I knew, I was only trying to do my job. "Give Austin and Grace a great program?"

The sarcasm bled through my words, and her heavily-made-up eyes narrowed. "You're trying to break Austin and Grace up."

Break them up? Did she mean romantically or as a skating partnership? Both ideas were ridiculous. They weren't actually dating, for one thing, and for another, Austin would never leave Grace to skate with me again. It wasn't even a possibility.

"I don't know what you're..." I started to say, but she cut me off by shoving her phone in my face.

It took me a second to focus on the screen, but eventually I saw them: a dozen or so photos of Austin and me at the sushi restaurant the night before, talking and laughing, and looking, I had to admit, pretty cozy with each other.

It could easily be mistaken for a date.

It kind of had been.

"How do you think Grace felt when she saw these?" Mrs Black demanded, and my stomach sank.

If Grace saw them, she would know that Austin lied to her about staying in his room to eat, and she would have found out right as they were going into their competition. The exact scenario we were trying to avoid.

"And the judges?" Mrs Black continued, not giving me a chance to respond at all. "Do you think they like the idea of my son cheating on his girlfriend?"

"Austin and Grace aren't dating," I pointed out, pushing her hand down to get the phone out of my face. The concept of personal space was apparently foreign to her.

"Everyone thinks they are," she countered just as firmly. "And now they think something has happened, that there's some kind of problem between them because he's out with someone else instead."

Almost without thinking, my head snapped back to the girls who had been staring at me earlier. Were these photos the reason for their attention? Did people really pay that much attention to Austin's private life? Who had taken the photos? Those kinds of things hadn't been much of a consideration for us back when we skated together, but we were both a lot younger then, and not nearly as well known.

Mrs Black stepped closer to me, the usual cold look in her eye she seemed to reserve exclusively for me. "I don't know exactly what you thought you were going to get out of this little stunt, but I am going to take care of it, like I always take care of my son. If you know what's good for you, you'll stay away from Austin and out of the spotlight for the rest of this trip."

"You can't tell me what to do," I shot back, my anger growing with every word she uttered. This woman ended my partnership with Austin, against both of our wishes, and she had the nerve to stand there threatening me? "I'm not a child who's scared of you anymore, Cynthia."

Her face turned red as I called her by her first name, but I was just getting warmed up.

"If Austin decides that it's any of your business, he can tell you why we were having dinner together last night. All I'm going to say is that I'm here to help him and Grace, and that's all. I'm not breaking anyone up, or plotting or scheming anything. That's your game, not mine."

She opened her mouth to reply, but I hadn't finished yet.

"Austin doesn't need you to take care of him. He's a grown man who is capable of running his own life and making his own decisions. And if he wants to take me out to dinner, that's absolutely none of your business either. Grow up, and leave me the hell alone."

Turning on my heel, I walked away from her and the ice, heading straight out to a taxi that would take me back to the hotel. In the back seat of the car, my hands shook and my heart raced from the adrenaline rush that surged through me from finally speaking my mind to the woman who had taken so much from me.

It felt damn good to tell her off, even if it was only a fraction of what she deserved.

But as my anger simmered back under control, I couldn't help wondering if I had just made things worse. The last thing Austin and Grace needed at this point was drama, and declaring war on Mrs Black hardly seemed like the way to avoid it.

And what about the photos? If Grace had already seen them, would Austin decide to come clean with her earlier than planned? The idea both pleased and worried me at the same time. I wanted to be with him so much, but not at the cost of damaging his career. If Grace was really as sensitive as he said, who could say how this would affect her?

Their on-ice success mattered more than anything, at least for now. If we could both keep that in mind, hopefully we could still get through this weekend unscathed.

~Austin~

My day had gone from bad to worse. First came Ben hanging around Amy again in the morning during our practice. Even though I trusted her when she said she wanted to be with me, I couldn't help the old resentment that bubbled up at the thought of him. I could call it jealousy, and in a way, it was, but that jealousy stemmed not so much from being jealous of him as a person as being envious of the way he always seemed to be so free to go after what he wanted.

Something I had never been with Amy.

After our morning practice, Grace and I had to do a few media appearances where she insisted on sitting so close to me, she may as well have been in my lap. A few times, she reached over and put her hand on my knee as she spoke, implying a level of intimacy that simply didn't exist between us. As much as I wanted to push it away, I couldn't do so in front of the cameras without everyone noticing and she must have known that.

I had been complaining about exactly that type of thing to Amy the night before: the way that Grace leaned into the pretense of our relationship more than necessary. Knowing I actually wanted to be with someone else instead made it even harder to stomach.

Once we got back to the hotel, I couldn't find Amy. I sent a series of texts to try to track her down, wanting to warn her about how those interviews might look, when a loud knock on my door interrupted me. As soon as I opened the door, all hell broke loose.

"You told me you were resting last night," Grace cried, her eyes red as she showed me the photos on her phone. "And you said you weren't dating her. This is exactly what I was worried about when you wanted to bring her in to work with us, and you said it wouldn't happen. You lied to me, Austin."

My stomach sank as I got a look at the pictures of me and Amy at the restaurant. I hadn't noticed anyone taking photos of us, but then, I hadn't been paying much attention to anything *other* than Amy. The world could have been falling apart around us and I probably wouldn't have noticed.

Meanwhile, Grace stood at my door, on the verge of a full meltdown, and we were meant to be leaving for the rink in less than an hour. Telling her the truth at that moment would be like setting off a bomb in the middle of our competition, so I told another lie instead.

"I changed my mind about going out and you'd already gone down to the restaurant. Amy happened to be available. You can see for yourself in the photos, we were just talking."

That hadn't been all I *wanted* to do, but given that our dinner didn't end up being all that private, I thanked my lucky stars that things hadn't gone any further than that.

"It's all over the forums," she moaned, flipping through pages on her phone. I couldn't be sure if she'd even heard a word I said. "Everyone's wondering what I did wrong and why you prefer this other girl to me."

"I wish you wouldn't read those things," I said, not for the first time. She got such a high off the praise she found, but the criticism always hit her hard. It would be better if she just didn't read any of it. "It doesn't matter what people are talking about. We just need to skate well."

The conversation went round in circles, and by the time we got to the arena, Grace's mood had only gotten worse. If people didn't think we were fighting before, they would after watching her sulk off to the locker room.

Another voice stopped me as I headed to my changing room. "Austin?"

Suppressing a groan, I turned around. I seriously could not catch a break today. "What are you doing here, Mom? Go up to the stands."

Since she wasn't part of the coaching team, she should have been watching the practice from the seating area, like the rest of the public.

"We need to talk about Amy," she started, but I cut her off immediately, not in any mood for her take on things.

"Not now. This is my practice time. If you don't leave, I'm getting security."

Her lips tightened, but to my surprise, she didn't argue. Something in my tone must have convinced her I wasn't messing around.

I needed to remember how I did that.

By the time Grace and I took to the ice for our practice, she would still hardly look at me. Trying to keep my face neutral, I pulled her close and whispered in her ear. "If you don't want people talking about what's wrong between us, don't act like there's something wrong."

That finally seemed to get through to her and she behaved more normally for the rest of the practice. I could have sworn I saw Amy at the boards when we went out, but by the time the practice ended, she was nowhere to be seen.

Technically, she didn't have to be there since we'd been focusing on the rhythm dance, but I always appreciated her input, not to mention seeing her face would have lifted my spirits when I really needed it.

Once I had changed back into my street clothes, I sent her a text, a repeat of the last one I'd sent her earlier that day.

> Where are you?

Her response came back quickly, at least.

> Back at the hotel. Is everything okay?

I could guess what her question referred to.

> You've seen the photos?

> Yes. How's Grace?

I told Amy exactly what I had said to Grace, and for a long time, no reply came. Eventually, I sent another message.

> We're heading back to the hotel now. Do you want to get something to eat?

> I've already ordered room service. I think the jet lag has caught up with me, I'm going to have an early night. See you tomorrow.

With a sigh, I shoved the phone back into my pocket as Grace came up beside me, and together, we got onto the shuttle bus that transported the athletes between the arena and the hotel.

As we walked down the aisle to grab some seats, Grace sneezed loudly.

Everyone around us immediately flinched, several of them covering their mouths and noses with their arms. Getting a cold could be disastrous during the season, and a lot of skaters were very strict about staying away from anyone who showed any sign of illness.

"Are you sick?" I whispered to her as we sat down beside each other, keeping my voice down so no one else would overhear.

She shook her head sullenly, obviously still angry with me. "I feel fine. Must have just been dust or something."

I hoped that was true. The day had been bad enough without anything else going wrong.

The next day was our rhythm dance, the first competition day. I started the morning with a workout in the hotel gym before knocking on Amy's door on my way back to my room to get changed.

No one answered.

With a frown, I pulled out my phone and sent her another text. Ever since we arrived in Japan, she felt further away from me than ever. I didn't want to sound like a broken record, so I started with something simple instead.

> Good morning.

Her reply came quickly.

> Hey. I'm with Brian, reviewing the training videos. Do you need me?

My mouth twitched, the first smile that had tempted me in a full twenty-four hours. Several different answers to that question flashed through my mind, none of them appropriately professional. In the end, I stuck to business.

> No, just curious what you were up to. I'm going to shower after my workout, I'll see you at lunch.

After my shower, I went to Grace's door, hoping she would be in a better mood that morning.

I could hear her sneeze again before she opened the door. "Are you coming down with something?" I asked as soon as she appeared. Sneezing that much wasn't typical for her. After spending pretty much every day with her for the last four years, I should know. Her hair was pulled back into its usual competition-day ponytail but she didn't have makeup on yet and I could see the telltale redness around her nose.

"Maybe a small cold," she admitted. "But it's fine, I'll get through it and I'll try not to breathe on you."

That would be difficult, considering how close we had to be during our dance, but if she said she felt well enough to skate, I trusted her. She knew her own body.

"Do you want to come down to lunch?"

Grace glanced over her shoulder, back into her room. "I just need another minute or two. I can meet you down there."

"Do you have company?" Something in the way she turned made me think someone else might be there, though I couldn't see anyone from my vantage point.

Grace bit her lip as though she might deny it, but in the end, she came clean. "I'm just chatting with your mom."

Sure enough, the woman in question came around the corner of the room once she'd been outed.

"What are you doing here?" I asked, my back already up. I had managed to avoid her after our brief altercation at the arena the night before, but I could guess what she and Grace had been discussing.

"Looking after your sick partner, like you should be doing."

My jaw clenched as I gritted my teeth to stop the words I *wanted* to say from getting out. Grace wasn't my responsibility off the ice. A grown woman should be able to handle a cold by herself, and even so, hadn't I just come to check on her?

It seemed far more likely that her presence in Grace's room had something to do with the photos of me and Amy. If we were alone, I could have said those things to my mother, but I didn't want to argue about Grace in front of her. Grace seemed to be less upset than she had been the day before and I certainly didn't want to set her off again.

"Grace says she's okay," I pointed out as calmly as I could. "Why don't we all go down to lunch?"

The rest of our group had already arrived by the time we got there. Amy, Brian and Kevin sat at one end of the table, talking about the programs, while Grace's parents were at the opposite end. Although I wanted to sit next to Amy, it would probably be safer not to until things were resolved. I sat next to Mr Matthews instead, who greeted me coolly.

The whole atmosphere at the table felt decidedly chilly. Nobody brought up the photos specifically, but they were clearly weighing on everyone's minds, and Grace kept sniffing, though she tried to hide it.

As everyone stood to leave, I finally managed to steal a few seconds with Amy. "What are you doing this afternoon? Do you want to go out for a walk? I could really do with getting out of here for a while."

Amy glanced behind me, where the rest of our group lingered. "I don't think that's a good idea."

I groaned in frustration, and Amy winced but held her ground.

"You know I'm right. If you're still hiding this from Grace, we can't be hanging out together. Being seen with me one time, you could explain, but if we went out for a walk now and people saw us..."

She didn't finish her thought, but she didn't have to. She was looking out for me, and I appreciated it, but I had really wanted to spend some time with her on this trip without having to be constantly looking over our shoulders.

"Do you want to just come hang out in my room then?" I offered. "No one will see us there."

Her sad smile tugged at my heart. "And what if Grace sees me coming out of your room? Or someone with a camera? I'm sorry, Austin, I just don't think it's a good idea. It's better if I go out for a while on my own, and you should get some rest anyway. I'll see you at the rink later."

She walked away before I could get another word out, leaving me even more frustrated than I had been before. *Another day and a half.* We just had to make it to the end of the free dance the next evening, and this whole ridiculous situation could finally be behind us for good.

Chapter Five

~**Amelia**~

Walking away from Austin after he asked me to go to his room with him might have been one of the hardest things I ever had to do.

I wanted to go with him. In fact, I *desperately* wanted to go with him. Ever since we found each other again, we hadn't been properly alone aside from that brief car ride to the airport, and the idea of what might happen when we finally managed to get some privacy had occupied more than a few of my daydreams lately.

And yet, I had to be realistic.

As much as he said he wanted to be with me, he didn't feel ready to tell Grace about us yet. When he texted me the night before to say he had lied to her again after the photos came out, my disappointment hit me harder than I expected it to. It almost felt like I'd become the mistress, waiting for my lover to leave his wife, and I didn't like being in that position.

For that reason most of all, I forced myself to walk away, reminding myself that we only had to wait one more day. After the free dance, after the competition ended, they would have that talk and we could go on our date, just like he promised. Until then, I'd just have to find another way to occupy my time.

Remembering that I'd seen a nearby park on the map we were given when we checked in, I stepped out the front door of the hotel, planning to head in that direction, and almost ran straight into Ben.

"I'm going to start thinking you're following me around pretty soon," he teased as we both took a step back, putting some space between us after our near-collision. His cheeks were tinged red from the cool temperature outside, his breath puffing out into the chilly air.

"This is my hotel, so maybe you're following me," I teased him back. "Are you staying here too?"

I hadn't seen him around at all, but that didn't mean anything. The hotel had several floors.

"No, we're just up the street, along with most of the other journalists." He pointed at a tall building in the distance with a hotel chain logo on the side. "I just came by to drop something off for Emily Marks at the front desk, she left it in the broadcast studio last night."

I'd noticed Emily, the top ladies single skater at the competition, in the restaurant on my way out. "I think she's still eating. I can go with you and check."

"That would be great."

Together, we headed back inside and found Emily at a table with her family. Ben returned her lost bag, chatting with her just as easily as he did with me, before we both headed back to the lobby.

"So, where were you off to before I interrupted you?" he asked.

"Just going for a walk. There's no practice today, so I don't have much going on until the rhythm dance later."

"I've got a bit of time too before I need to get back for the men's competition. Do you want some company?"

He had been good company the day before, so I accepted his offer and we headed out towards the park.

FIGURING IT OUT

"So, how does it feel to be 'just' the choreographer?" he asked with his usual teasing tone of voice once we reached the open space, the birds singing in the trees making it easy to forget we were still in a huge, busy city.

"What?"

It didn't necessarily sound like an insult, but it was still an odd way to phrase it if he wanted to ask how I felt about not skating at the event.

"Grace's post?" he followed up, and when I continued to stare at him blankly, he chuckled. "You still don't do social media, eh? I should have guessed. I tried to look you up the other day and couldn't find any accounts for you."

None of his words made any sense to me. "Grace posted something?" I asked, trying to figure out what I'd missed.

Pulling the glove off his hand, he reached into his pocket and grabbed his phone, accessing Grace's Instagram profile with a few quick taps. The first photo showed her looking out her hotel window in her bathrobe, a cup of coffee in her hand, no doubt meant to look like she'd just woken up even though her hair and makeup were already done.

The caption read: *Lazy start to the morning in Tokyo for me and Austin. Thanks for all your messages of support but there's nothing to worry about, she's just our choreographer. See you all later for the RD!*

My blood boiled from the first line. Obviously, she meant to imply that Austin had taken the photo of her, that they were together in her room, but that couldn't be true. Someone else must have taken it, and that blatant attempt to manipulate everyone's perceptions bothered me far more than the 'just our choreographer' comment.

That was exactly what Austin had complained about to me at the dinner the other night, and that post made it clearer than ever.

"Someone's a bit threatened by you," Ben laughed as he took the phone back from me. "I don't miss all the drama around the rink, I can tell you that. It's like high school but worse."

I tried to smile back at him, pushing against the anger I felt. It would be nice to confide in Ben, to tell him the truth about Austin and Grace, but I had to remember that, as nice as he was, he still had a job to do. I'd have to choose my words carefully.

"I guess you saw the pictures of me and Austin having supper the other day? It seems like there were some rumours after those came out, so she's probably just trying to put a stop to them."

In a particularly underhanded way, I added in my head.

"If you want to stop those rumours, there are other ways to go about it," he suggested mildly.

I didn't have a clue what that meant. "How would I do that?"

"Well, you could always take a photo with someone else to show that you being out with Austin is no big deal. Maybe someone like a former-skater-turned-journalist who has a pretty decent social media following too?"

"You?" I squeaked in surprise. "You want to get involved in this? You just said you don't miss the drama!"

He laughed at the dismay in my tone. "One photo is hardly 'getting involved'. I've been posting pictures with people all week. I can post one of us and say something like, 'Exploring Tokyo with Mia Wilson, choreographer to Matthews and Black.' That'll tell people who you are, what your connection with Austin is, and that you're hanging out with people other than him too. What do you think?"

That... might actually work. It could take some of the pressure off Austin for the rest of the weekend and let him focus on their competition, where his attention *should* be.

"You're sure you don't mind?"

He shrugged with a confident indifference. "It's just a picture. And if you're asking if I have a problem with the world seeing me out with a beautiful girl? Definitely not."

My cheeks flushed at the compliment even as I told myself to grow up. What was it about both him and Austin that made me revert to being the shy teenager I used to be all over again? Other men could compliment me without me turning beet red, but for some reason, when the two men who had known me in my former life said things like that, it felt different and I reacted differently too.

Ben awaited my answer with an encouraging smile, and the more I thought about it, the more it made sense to me. "Let's do it," I agreed. "One picture, and hopefully that'll put the whole thing to rest."

~**Austin**~

By the time we left for the rink, Grace looked terrible. Her nose had turned raw and red from blowing it so much, and her eyes watered as she dabbed at them with a Kleenex, trying to stop her mascara from running.

We were going to have to tell people about her cold or they would think she'd been crying over those stupid photos of me and Amy.

As usual, neither of us looked at our phones as we got ready to go out on the ice. When we came out for our warm-up, Amy and Brian stood huddled together, whispering about something, and when they saw us, they both put on smiles that looked a little *too* bright. I got the distinct feeling that something was going on, but I also suspected they wouldn't tell us about it until after the competition, so as not to distract us. Therefore, I did my best to put it out of my mind and focus on the task at hand.

Grace had caked on a few extra layers of make-up to try to hide her illness, but she also kept blowing her nose during the warm-up, rubbing off most of the make-up around her nose in the process and making it look even redder in contrast to the rest of her face.

Somehow, we made it through the warm-up and came back off the ice. We were the second team to skate in our group, so we didn't go far, moving around to keep ourselves loose. As the first team came off the ice, we went back on to get warmed up again while the other team got their marks.

As we stroked hand-in-hand around the rink, Grace swayed into me, nearly losing her balance.

"Are you alright?"

Genuine concern laced my voice. This seemed worse than a little cold, leaving me wondering if she could even make it through the program.

"It's fine," she quickly assured me. "I got dizzy for a second, but I'm fine now. It's okay."

"Grace..." The word lingered between us like a warning. Her being dizzy during a dance where I had to spin her around more than once could be a recipe for disaster.

"Seriously. I'm fine." Her voice came out firmer and her eyes met mine, steely with determination. "We already lost our non-scoring event because we were working on the new program. We need this. We can't pull out."

"We *can* pull out if you're going to hurt yourself," I countered. "The last thing we need is either of us getting injured. This event isn't worth that. Getting to the Grand Prix final isn't worth it."

She glanced away from me, towards the boards where Brian and Amy stood together, watching us, and her lips tightened. "I'll make it through," she insisted, and I had little choice but to trust her.

Our names were called and we skated to the centre of the ice, taking our starting position. My heart beat fast with more than the usual adrenaline as I waited for the opening beats of the music, having no idea how this dance was going to go.

At the end of the two and a half minutes, we were still on our feet, but I couldn't think of much else positive to say about it. Grace had stepped out of her twizzles on the straight-line step sequence, and more than once, I'd had to pull her closer to me as she drifted off the line during our other steps.

We couldn't pretend it had been a good performance, and I could see it clearly on Amy's face as we came off the ice.

"What's wrong? Are you okay?" Amy whispered to Grace, trying to speak directly to her about it, but Grace shook her head to indicate she didn't want to talk and walked away to the kiss 'n' cry.

Amy and I exchanged glances, but I couldn't explain it to her at that moment, having no choice but to follow Grace to where the cameras waited.

In all honesty, the marks weren't as bad as they could have been. The judges seemed to have given us a bit of leeway in the presentation components, leaving us third after the rhythm dance, and still within striking distance of the leading team. Still, we would need a much better performance the next day, and if Grace didn't feel up to it, we would *have* to withdraw.

Pulling out would be better than putting in another performance like that.

The usual reporters waited for us backstage as we headed back to the locker rooms. "Do you want to skip this?" I whispered in Grace's ear.

She shook her head. "No. I'll have to explain."

We went to the American network first and the reporter wasted no time in asking us what happened during our performance.

"I'm not feeling very well," Grace admitted with a shaky smile. "It came on pretty suddenly, so hopefully it'll pass quickly too. I'm sure tomorrow will be better."

I offered a supportive smile in the background, saying nothing until the reporter turned to me.

"We're all looking forward to seeing your new free dance tomorrow. What has it been like working with your old partner, Amy Gardiner?"

If anyone had ever looked like a deer caught in the headlights, it would have been me at that moment. The lights of the camera seemed to blind me as I blinked slowly, my heart thudding slow and heavy in my chest.

How did she know about Amy? We'd credited her as Mia, just as she wanted. I hadn't let anything slip, I knew I hadn't.

My mind raced, the only part of me that seemed capable of doing anything as the shock coursed through my body.

Finally, I swallowed, realizing my mouth had fallen open at some point, and tried to keep my composure as I stared down at the microphone in front of me, waiting to pick up my response.

"Our... uh, our new free dance is really... uh... really great, and we're excited for everyone to see it."

Whatever the reporter asked next, I missed it, simply nodding and smiling while Grace said something else. From there, we moved next to Ben with the Canadian network who stuck to asking us about the performance. Amy didn't come up again.

When he finished, I pulled Grace past the rest of the reporters without answering any other questions. As soon as we were alone, she turned to me, her face tight and her eyes watering again. "Why are they asking about her? This is supposed to be about us, Austin! I knew this would happen! You said it wouldn't, but now everyone knows."

She grabbed another Kleenex, blowing her nose loudly while my jaw clenched, my whole body still numb with shock.

What the hell had I missed?

~**Amelia**~

As soon as Austin and Grace walked away from the kiss 'n' cry, I realized that I'd been so distracted by Grace's illness and their overall performance that I completely forgot to warn them about the *other* thing that happened since I'd arrived at the rink.

The fact that my 'secret' identity had been revealed and everyone knew exactly who I was.

I rushed down the hall after them, but it quickly became apparent that I was too late. They were already speaking to a reporter and as soon as I got within earshot, I heard her ask Austin about working with me.

For just a second, he froze. My heart contracted in response, wishing I could do something to help, hating that I'd put him in that position, but like a consummate professional, he recovered quickly. People who didn't know him probably wouldn't guess just how much the question blindsided him. They might even chalk up his stumbling answer to the subpar performance they'd just put in and the disappointment he must have been feeling over it.

Thankfully, when they moved on to Ben, he didn't ask them anything about me, and after that, they skipped the rest of the reporters, heading straight to the locker room.

I tried to sneak past the reporters to follow them, but luck remained stubbornly against me. "Ms Gardiner," the American reporter called out to me. "Amy. Can we ask you a couple of questions?"

Should I speak to them? I still didn't want any attention, but maybe if I addressed the questions, they wouldn't bother Austin and Grace about it again.

Maybe I could try to make up for all of this getting out of hand.

My biggest mistake had been completely underestimating how resourceful skating fans could be. When Ben posted the picture of the two of us that afternoon, they jumped on it, as he'd anticipated. At first, the comments were exactly what we'd hoped for.

Oh, that makes sense! That must be why she was with Austin.
I knew he wouldn't cheat on Grace.

A few of the comments speculated on whether Ben and I were a couple. Perhaps I should have anticipated that, but it didn't concern me too much. Austin knew the truth, and it didn't matter to me what anyone else thought.

However, all my plans to stop the rumours came to a screeching end when someone posted a simple question that set off a firestorm of new comments.

Doesn't she kind of look like Amy Gardiner? Whatever happened to her?

Soon, people were sharing old photos of me, comparing my face in Ben's picture with photos of me and Austin during our competitive appearances. It didn't take long before the consensus was in: Mia Wilson and Amy Gardiner were one and the same.

A whole new crop of rumours began to swirl around. Were Austin and I getting back together on the ice? Were we dating? Why was I in disguise? Why did I go by a different name?

I'd only become aware of all of this when I got to the rink, since I still didn't use social media at all myself, a holdover from my mom's insistence on keeping me off it when I was younger. Brian filled me in when I arrived, since people had already been asking him about it, and we both agreed it would be better not to tell Austin and Grace about the whole situation until after they'd skated.

Which I meant to do, until they had that less-than-stellar skate, and now, things were even more out of control.

"I can answer one or two questions," I agreed hesitantly as the reporter and the cameraman got closer to me.

"Great." The reporter smiled at me before turning back to the cameraman, waiting for his signal. Once she got it, she turned back to me. "We're here with former World Junior champion, and Austin Black's former dance partner, Amy Gardiner. Amy, we've just learned today that you're choreographing a new program for Austin and Grace. How did that come about?"

I tried to answer as honestly as possible without going into too many details. "Austin and I recently reconnected and he asked me to join their team to help with their free dance. We're all excited for them to debut it here tomorrow."

"We're all excited to see it," she agreed smoothly. "And what's it like to work with your old partner and his new partner? It must be a bit like when your ex-husband gets remarried."

She laughed and I tried to keep the smile on my face too, and not to show just how close to home that comment hit. "We're all focused on making sure Austin and Grace have the best program possible. They're the best dancers in the world, and hopefully, this program is going to prove that. Thank you."

I moved away before she could ask anything else, my stomach still twisting slightly from that ex-husband comparison.

By the time I got to the locker room, Brian and Mrs Black were already there. Tension sat heavy in the air. I hadn't spoken to Mrs Black since our argument the night before, and she glared at me as I came in.

"All that matters right now is the competition," Austin was saying, making me think that they'd been talking about something else before I got there. He glanced over at me but he didn't stop talking. "We'll see how Grace feels in the morning."

My eyes went to Grace, whose nose and eyes were even more red than they had been on the ice. She really didn't look well at all.

Austin turned to her too, his voice softening as he spoke to her directly. "If you're not feeling up to it, we'll withdraw. It's not the end of the world."

"But then we won't qualify for the Grand Prix final," she pointed out, sniffling as she spoke, though I couldn't tell if her runny nose came from her cold or her emotions. "We won't have any other international competitions before the Olympics."

Austin shrugged. "Then we'll deal with that. You can't force yourself to skate in this condition, Grace, and you can't force your body to get better. We'll just have to see what happens."

"Let's not stress about it until we know what the morning brings," Brian suggested, clearly trying to wrap up the conversation. "Get changed and we'll head back to the hotel. I'll get a taxi so you don't have to go on the bus. Mia, can I see you for a second?"

He led me away from the room as Austin and Grace left to go get changed. A short way down the hall, he turned to me.

"I don't actually need to talk to you, I just wanted to get you away from Cynthia."

"She's that mad, huh?"

I could have anticipated that. She must be livid about the attention being directed at me. Anything that drew attention away from Austin always infuriated her, and when the attention went to me instead, it was even worse.

"It's all a bit of a mess." Brian ran a hand through his hair, and a pang of sympathy for him tightened my chest. He'd worked as hard for this competition as anyone and he didn't deserve this mess any more than Austin did. "Look, it's up to you how you want to handle this, but I think now that the story's out there, it might be better if we try to get ahead of it. Tell your side of the story before rumours get really out of hand."

I nodded as I thought it over. That did make sense, especially since I didn't have anything to hide anymore. "I already answered a few questions, but there's someone who I could get to sit down with me to tell the whole story, if you think it will help."

"Only if you're comfortable with it, but I really do think it's best to just get it all out there so we can all move on. If we can even perform tomorrow."

I nodded once again. When it came to Grace's health, I couldn't be of much help, but at least I could try to staunch the other rumours and make things easier for them that way. "I'll make my own way back to the hotel. I'll see you tomorrow."

After he walked away, I went in search of Ben. It didn't take long to find him, still standing in the hall near the locker rooms, waiting for some of the other skaters to finish.

He gave me a sympathetic smile as I approached. "That didn't really go as planned, did it?"

I didn't know if he meant Austin and Grace's program or the reaction to the photo we'd taken together, but it didn't really matter. Both were true.

"Not really, but I'm wondering if you could help me with something else."

His expression turned curious. "What is it?"

I took a deep breath, trying to steel myself to revisit my painful past one more time, this time in public. "How would you like to write the exclusive story of exactly what happened to Amy Gardiner?"

Chapter Six

~Austin~

I barely had my skates off in the locker room before Brian came rushing in. "I didn't get a chance to tell you: everyone knows about Amy."

No kidding. "It would have been helpful to know that *before* being asked about it in front of a camera," I gritted out while Grace continued to dab at her eyes with her Kleenex.

Hot on our coach's heels, my mom stormed in. "I hope you're happy now, Austin! That girl just sabotaged you in the middle of a competition. Everyone's talking about her. I knew she was up to no good."

"Sabotage?" I spat the word out, the taste of it on my tongue too vile to keep it in. "All she's done is work incredibly hard for the last four weeks to give us the best program she can."

It couldn't have been easy for her to be there, watching Grace do all the things she used to do, knowing that, by rights, it should have been her out there on the ice. Despite that, she hadn't done a single thing that could remotely be classified as sabotage. I just wish I knew what she *had* been doing.

Amy herself walked in at that point, and I quickly changed the subject. Brian took her away before I had a chance to ask her exactly what happened, and I kicked my mom out so I could finish changing. By the time I got ready, Grace and my mom were huddled together, speaking quietly. Grace had her skates off but she hadn't changed out of her costume.

"I just want to get back to my room," she sniffed when she saw me glancing down at her clothing as I approached. "I want to get out of here."

Brian joined us a moment later. "The car's here. Let's go."

I glanced around, not seeing the one person I wanted to talk to more than anything. "Where's Amy?"

Both Grace and my mother tensed at the sound of her name and Brian ushered them towards the door as he turned to me. "She'll join us back at the hotel later," he told me under his breath, clearly not wanting to stir things up any further.

The awkward taxi ride was silent other than Grace's occasional sniffles. When we got back to the hotel, I walked Grace to her room, away from my mother and everyone else.

"Get some rest. I'll come check on you in the morning, and if you're not feeling any better, we'll pull out. I mean it. It's not worth it."

"I'll be feeling better," she promised stiffly. "Don't worry."

She closed the door in my face and I let out a long sigh. This stubbornness wasn't usual for her. We'd pulled out of competitions before. Sure, doing it in an Olympic year wouldn't be the best timing, but it wouldn't be the end of the world either, though Grace seemed to think so.

Only a minute or so after I let myself into my own room, someone knocked at the door. My heart leapt, hoping to find Amy on the other side, but instead, when I opened it, my mom stood there, her lips drawn tightly together.

"We need to talk, Austin."

Without waiting for a reply, she pushed past me, striding into the room and I rolled my eyes once behind her back before closing the door and turning to face her.

"If you're going to continue with your ridiculous conspiracy theories about Amy, then no, we don't. You can leave right now."

"When are you going to wake up and see that girl for what she really is?" she demanded. "What she's always been?"

"And what has she 'always been'?" I asked, crossing my arms as I waited for her response. This ought to be good.

"An overrated, attention-grabbing diva who cares only about herself," came her ludicrous reply.

Disbelief dripped through my body as I stared at the woman in front of me. "I truly don't understand this hatred you have for her. I would never be where I am today if it wasn't for her. You know that. Grace and I were going nowhere when I chose to skate with Amy. I was damn lucky that she picked me, and she made me a better skater and a better partner than I could have ever become without her. Her influence and what she taught me helped me bring Grace up to this level too."

My mom opened her mouth to respond, but I kept going before she could get a word out, my anger rising with each word.

"You lied to me to end our partnership, and continued to lie to me about it for four years. And when she finally comes back, putting aside any grudge that she would have every right to bear and gives up four weeks of her life to design a killer free dance for us, you think she's somehow trying to *sabotage* me? Do you even hear how insane that sounds?"

"Are you in love with her?"

The question came out of nowhere, so far from what we were talking about, that for a moment I could only stare at her, trying to wrap my head around it. "What?"

"You heard me." Her voice sounded cold, but I could sense the barely repressed fury lurking just behind it. "Is that what this is about? Do you think you're in love with her?"

"That is even less of your business than what happens on the ice." In no world could I imagine discussing my feelings for Amy with my mother. I wouldn't have wanted to do it at the best of times, let alone after what she just said.

"It *is* my business if she's leading you on. You haven't seen the photo, have you?"

I didn't know what photo she meant, and it must have shown on my face because her lips twisted into a smug smile.

"I didn't think so. This is why everyone knows who she is now. And if you think she didn't plan it that way, you're being incredibly naïve."

She pulled out her phone, the screen already displaying an Instagram post from earlier that day. A photo of Amy and Ben stared back at me, the two of them outside somewhere, smiling at the camera with his arm around her.

Was that where she went that afternoon instead of spending time with me like I'd asked her to?

A bitter stew of anger and jealousy bubbled up in my stomach before I could stop it, but I refused to give my mom the satisfaction of letting it show. Deep down, I knew that Amy would never go back on her word to me, and I refused to let my mom try to manipulate me into thinking otherwise.

"You were upset yesterday because there were pictures of her with me. Today, you're upset because there's a picture of her with someone else. Is there anything she could do that *wouldn't* upset you?"

My mom muttered something under her breath, and my blood turned cold, icy shock spreading through my veins as I realized just how hateful she could be.

It sounded very much like 'crawl back into the hole she was hiding in.'

"Do you want to repeat that?"

As if scales had finally fallen from my eyes, letting me see her clearly for the first time, I took a step back from my mother in disgust. Had she really always been like this? Had I just been that blind to it?

Some of my emotion must have shown on my face, because my mom immediately backed down. "It was nothing," she mumbled.

"It didn't sound like nothing to me. It sounded like your last chance going up in smoke. I warned you, Mom. I told you if you didn't back off Amy, you were finished, and I meant it. But you just couldn't help yourself, could you?"

"Austin, I..."

"No. No more chances. You're fired. You're not my manager anymore, you're not my publicist, you have absolutely no reason to be anywhere near me."

Her response rushed out of her lips, immediate and predictable. "You don't mean that, Austin. I'm just trying to protect you, you need me..."

"I. Don't. Need. You."

I spoke slowly and clearly so there could be no way she didn't hear or understand me.

"I don't need your help or your protection, or whatever you think this is. All I've ever really needed was your support, but it always came with all these strings attached, and I'm tired of it. If you want to come to the free dance tomorrow, you can buy a ticket and sit in the stands like everyone else. You're not welcome in the locker room and you're not welcome at the rink when we get home. You thought you were banished before? Now, you'll know what it really feels like. It's over."

I went and opened the door, standing by it until she made her way over. She tried to catch my eye again as she reached me, but I shook my head, refusing to look at her.

"Go. I've got nothing else to say to you."

Once she stepped out into the hall, I closed and locked the door behind her before grabbing a pillow off the bed and screaming into it, trying to channel all of my frustration into that innocent piece of bedding. Everything seemed to be falling apart. We weren't skating well and everyone was at each other's throats, right when we needed to be in sync more than ever before.

Was the universe punishing me for everything I did wrong with Amy?

What could I do to fix it?

With her at the front of my mind, I left my room and went down the hall to Amy's room, knocking several times with no answer. She must have still been on her way back from the arena, but sitting in my room waiting wouldn't accomplish anything. Needing some kind of release, I went down to the hotel gym and ran off my frustration on the treadmill, my feet pounding into the machine and sweat dripping into my eyes.

Half an hour later, I returned to Amy's door, but still, no one answered the door.

Grabbing my phone from my pocket, I sent the same text I kept sending her since we arrived in Japan.

> Where are you?

I watched the screen until the dots began to bounce, letting me know she was typing.

However, when the reply came, I felt like screaming all over again.

> I'm with Ben, not sure yet when I'll be back. Don't wait up for me.

~Amelia~

I put my phone down after replying to Austin's text, guilt gnawing at my stomach. I wanted to be there with him, talking about what happened both with me and with their performance, but in the long run, clearing the air publicly would probably be the better use of my time that evening.

"Everything okay?" Ben asked, taking a sip from his drink. He'd found us some comfortable seats at the bar at his hotel where we could sit and talk as he asked me all the questions he had for the article he planned to write.

"Everything's fine," I fibbed. Hopefully, it would be. "Where was I?"

"You were explaining that your injuries weren't the reason you stopped skating, even though everyone assumed so at the time. That's what I thought. But if that wasn't the reason, what was?"

As carefully as I could, I explained to him the series of events and misunderstandings that led to Austin and I both believing that the other person chose to end our partnership. I didn't specifically lay the blame on either of our mothers, even though they had both played a significant and deliberate role in the mix-up. Pointing fingers wouldn't help. Instead, I tried to make it clear that neither Austin nor I were at fault, trying to ensure that no one would take sides or blame one of us more than the other.

I also explained how we got back in touch through the article I wrote, which would be published the following month. The magazine would probably appreciate the plug.

Finally, I talked about how doing the article led to me helping Austin and Grace with their program, which explained my presence in Tokyo.

"What about the rumours that there's something going on between you and Austin?" Ben asked, still in his journalist mode. "People are speculating that that's the real reason that you're here."

If he asked me that when we were back in Canada, I could have told him the truth. However, since he intended to post his article first thing in the morning, before the free dance, I would have to keep up the deception a little longer.

"Austin and I have a professional relationship. His focus is on his skating, as it should be."

"Really?" Ben cocked an eyebrow at me, suddenly switching into his teasing, friendly style of conversation. "And what about off the record? You can tell me the truth, Mia. Is there something holding you back?"

I opened my mouth to ask him what he meant, but I didn't have to. Before I could say anything, he leaned forward, placed his hand on my cheek, and pressed his lips softly against mine.

For a second, I froze, unable to process what was happening. His lips were warm and slightly wet from the drink he'd just taken. The scent of his cologne filled my nose, and though it smelled nice enough, it didn't do anything to my stomach like Austin's always did.

As my brain kicked back into gear, I pulled back, my eyes wide with surprise as I stared at him. "Ben, I'm sorry, I can't... I didn't mean to suggest..."

He cut me off, a resigned smile on his face. "I had a feeling that was the case, but I wanted to be sure."

His words made no more sense to me than his actions did. "What?"

"I think the same thing would have happened if I actually went ahead and kissed you all those years ago too. Austin's a very lucky guy."

My mouth flapped open and closed a couple of times, trying to decide how to respond to that, and Ben chuckled, settling back into his seat.

"I've seen the way you look at him. It's always been him, hasn't it?"

He had no idea just how true those words were, and after what just happened, there didn't seem any point in hiding it. "It has. I'm sorry. Please don't tell anyone, we're not ready for anything to be public just yet. We're still figuring things out."

"I won't say a word, but don't apologize for the way you feel. I don't get why the two of you are hiding it. If I were him, I'd be shouting it from the rooftops."

Austin trying to appease Grace was a whole other story, and I had already taken up enough of his time for one night. "Have you got everything you need?" I asked, attempting to change the subject without any subtlety whatsoever.

Luckily, Ben didn't seem to mind, turning off his recorder with a knowing smile. "I think so. Thank you for trusting me with this, Mia. I'm probably going to stay up all night and finish it so I can post it tomorrow before the free dance. Everyone will be dying to read it, and I think you'll find you still have a lot more fans out there than you think you do. I'll come by in the morning to let you take a look first, if that's okay."

"That sounds perfect. Thank you."

"You're welcome. Come on, I'll walk you back to your hotel."

By the time he dropped me off at my door, it was nearly two in the morning. My eyes landed on Austin's door down the hall, wishing I could go and see him, but he would be fast asleep, resting up for the free dance the next day, and I couldn't disturb him, no matter how much I wanted to see him. Instead, I let myself into my own room and fell into a restless sleep.

Almost before I knew it, someone knocked at my hotel room door, and with a groan, I rolled over to see that the clock read 8:03. Normally, I would have been awake for a couple of hours already. When the knock sounded again, my heart sped up, thinking it might be Austin, and everything else came rushing back to me.

The free dance took place in just a few hours. By the time the day ended, we wouldn't need to hide anymore. Everything would be different.

Scrambling out of bed, I pulled the door open without even bothering to brush my hair or check my face, a wide smile ready to greet him, but I didn't find Austin on the other side. Instead, Ben stood there, looking far more awake than he had any right to be considering he probably got even less sleep than I did.

His expression immediately turned apologetic as he caught sight of me still in my pajamas. "I'm so sorry if I woke you. I was just so excited to get this posted."

He held up the laptop in his hands, which I could only assume contained the article he'd written in the time I'd been sleeping.

"It's okay," I mumbled, embarrassment rushing in that I hadn't made any effort to make myself presentable. At least it hadn't been Brian or, worse, Cynthia. "Come on in. I'll make some coffee, do you want some?"

Ben followed me into the room and handed me the laptop, telling me he would look after the coffee while I read. By the time I had my first sip, my mind had already fully switched on, thanks to Ben's excellent article. Extremely well written, it made my whole life sound way more dramatic and exciting than it actually was. Even I found myself rooting for the girl in the article, hoping that things worked out for her in the end.

"What do you think?" he asked as I took another long sip of my coffee.

"It's incredible. Almost *too* incredible. Won't people think you're being a bit biased?"

His warm laugh rumbled through the room. "It's an amazing story, Mia. You've been through a lot and you've overcome it all, and now you're using your talents to help the very person who put you through so much misery, intentional or not. That's inspirational. People will love it."

"You're sure it doesn't make Austin or Grace sound bad?" I pressed. I did this interview to try to fix the problems my presence had created for them, not cause any more speculation.

"Not at all," he assured me. "There are no villains in this story other than crossed wires."

And our mothers. That part, I kept to myself.

"If you're happy with it, I'm going to get it up on the website right away," he continued. "That way people can read it before the free dance and they'll all be rooting for Austin and Grace even more than before. And for you, of course."

"That sounds perfect."

We exchanged smiles as I handed the laptop back to him.

"I'm not sure if I'll see you at the rink today, but you've got my number if you need it," he said as we walked back over to the door of the room. "Give me a call if you need anything."

I gave him a quick hug, feeling lucky that I'd reconnected with him on this trip, in spite of the drama it had caused. "Thanks, Ben. I really appreciate all your support."

"Anytime, Mia." He pulled the door open before immediately stopping short, and it didn't take long to see what had stopped him.

Austin stood in the doorway, his hand raised as if he had been about to knock.

In his workout clothes, his hair slick with sweat and his shirt clinging to his chest, he must have just come from the gym. He looked as handsome as ever, but I could spot the dark spots under his eyes, suggesting he hadn't slept all that well either.

The two men stared at each other for a second before Austin's eyes moved to me, looking me up and down as he took in the just-woken-up state of me, my pajamas still on, no make-up, and my hair still a tangled mess. Confusion filled his gaze, along with a flash of hurt that nearly took my breath away.

Surely, he didn't think…

Well, what else *would* he think? We'd barely spoken in two days. The last thing I'd texted him the night before was that I was with Ben, and now, he found him leaving my hotel room in the morning.

I knew what I'd think.

"Hey, Austin, good morning," Ben said, his tone light as he did his best to smooth over any awkwardness. "I'm just leaving, but good luck with your dance today. Hope I can talk to you later after you guys win."

He edged past Austin, shooting me a sympathetic glance over his shoulder, and Austin's eyes never left me as Ben's footsteps echoed down the hall.

"It's not what it looks like," I said weakly, knowing just how cliché that sounded. "Please, come in. We need to talk."

~**Austin**~

By the time I finished in the gym that morning, I'd convinced myself that nothing was going on between Ben and Amy. Her text the night before threw me for a loop, I had to admit, but if we were going to be in a relationship, I needed to trust her. I *did* trust her. She knew how I felt about her, and even though we hadn't made any kind of formal commitment to each other yet, I believed that if she had any doubts, she would've told me.

So, overall, I'd been in a pretty decent mood when I went to knock on her door after my workout, looking forward to finally seeing her and talking through what happened the day before.

All of that flew out the window when the door to her room opened and Ben stood there with Amy next to him, still in her pajamas.

My mind went completely blank.

All the things I'd wanted to say to her abandoned me. Any thoughts I might have had about how cute she looked in her plaid flannel pajamas? Buried. All I could do was stare at them both as I tried to come up with any possible reason for him to be in her room other than the blatantly obvious one. Vaguely, I registered him saying something to me as he left, but my eyes stayed on Amy. She said things weren't what they looked like, but as much as I wanted that to be true, I didn't know how it could be. What else could it be?

Had I really lost her when we were so close to finally being together?

Only after she gave me a quizzical look did I realize she must have said something else too. "What?"

"Come in," she said, gesturing towards the room. "Please."

I only made it two steps into her room before catching sight of the unmade bed and my thoughts spiraled into even darker places.

Unable to entertain the thought for even another second, I spun back around to face her and blurted out the question drowning out everything else in my head. "Did you sleep with him?"

Amy's eyes widened, probably from the bluntness of my words as much as anything. She didn't have her glasses on yet, making it easier to see every emotion flickering in her gaze. "No! Of course not."

I gulped in a breath of air, trying to accept that answer at face value. "Then what...? I don't understand."

I didn't manage to get a full question out that time, but I didn't have to. She knew what I wanted to know. "He came over this morning from his hotel, ten minutes ago. I was still sleeping when he got here."

Nothing in her face or her voice suggested any of that was untrue, but pieces of the puzzle were still missing. "But you were with him last night."

"Yes. I spent some time talking to him last night, and afterwards, I came back and spent the night here, alone. This morning, he came over to finish our conversation." Her arms wrapped around her stomach as her mouth twisted, the first show of emotion since she let me into her room. "Do you really think I would do that, Austin? After everything we talked about the other night, and without talking to you first?"

"No, I don't." I sighed as I sank down onto the edge of her bed, dropping my head into my hands. I really didn't believe she would go behind my back, but after all the stress of the past few days, I'd reached my wit's end. And now, I'd upset her, the last thing I wanted to do. "I'm sorry, Amy. I know you better than that. I just feel like my head's going to explode, everything is so out of control right now."

Her expression instantly softened. "I know, and I understand what it looked like. I'm sorry, too, for not keeping you more up-to-date. Thank you for asking me directly, at least."

We shared a smile with those words, an understanding tinged with sadness. If only we'd just asked each other a few questions directly all those years ago, how different things might have been.

"There's more we need to talk about," Amy added as she took a seat next to me, keeping a little distance between us. "Ben's writing a story about me. About what happened to me with the accident and how I'm working with you now. That's what we were talking about last night and that's why he came here this morning. He wanted to let me read it before he posted it."

A fresh wave of relief washed over me as all the puzzle pieces came into focus. However, I still didn't understand one thing. "I thought you didn't want anyone to know who you are."

"I didn't, but it got out anyway after Ben posted the photo yesterday, so Brian and I thought it might be better to just get the whole story out there. Hopefully, that will satisfy everyone's curiosity and they'll go back to focusing on you and Grace, like they should be."

A deep exhale released all the tension from my body, leaving me feeling a hundred times lighter. "You should know by now that I don't mind people focusing on you. They will be anyway, once they see how good your program is."

"Well, your mom certainly doesn't agree with that," she said with a rueful smile and a touch of sarcasm in her tone.

If my mom had spoken to Amy directly, I could only imagine what she said, but at least on that point, I'd already taken action. "I fired her last night. You don't have to worry about her anymore."

Her eyes got even wider than they had before, genuine surprise lighting up her expression. "You really fired her?"

"I really did. She crossed the line. A long time ago, actually, but this was the final straw. So, yeah, I fired her. She doesn't have any say in anything I do, on or off the ice."

Amy took a deep breath of her own, her shoulders rising and falling inside her flannel pajamas. "That's a big change for you, Austin."

"An overdue one." I edged slightly closer to her, my thigh brushing lightly against hers. "It's time for me to really live my life the way *I* want to, and that includes being with you."

"You're definitely going to tell Grace today?" she asked, and even though she looked down at her hands rather than up at me, I could hear the hope underpinning the question anyway.

"I am. The first chance I get. As soon as the dance is over."

Her gaze remained fixed on her hands, her fingers pressing against each other in a rhythm all her own. "And you're really not worried about what the judges or anyone else thinks?"

"Your free dance is so good, I can't imagine it will make any difference whether people think Grace and I are together or not."

When she nodded without looking up, I reached over to hook her chin with my finger, forcing her head up until her blue eyes locked on mine.

"The only thing I know for sure is that when that door opened just now and I saw Ben standing there, I thought I'd lost you again and it crushed me. Not getting an Olympic medal would hurt less. If I had any doubt before, I know it now: you're my priority. I don't want to have to choose, and I don't see any reason I should have to, but if I do, you're my choice. I'm choosing you, Amy."

That gorgeous blush of hers spread across her cheeks, her lips breaking into a hopeful smile she couldn't contain. "Thank you."

"You don't have to thank me. I know you'd do the same. You *are* doing it, choosing to work with me even if it hurts not to be on the ice, choosing to give up your privacy to put the focus back on our performance. Don't think I haven't noticed. I see it, and I appreciate it."

We were so close by that point, it would have been so easy to lean down and kiss her and show her with more than just my words that I meant everything I said.

But before I could, Amy pulled away, getting to her feet, as if she didn't trust herself to sit next to me any longer. "Alright. First, let's get through today. Are you guys skating this afternoon? How's Grace?"

Clearing my throat to refocus myself, I pulled out my phone. "I'm actually not sure yet. I promised to check on her this morning. Let me give her a call."

I'd barely got the phone up to my ear when Grace picked up. "Hey. I just went to your room looking for you. Where are you?"

Thankfully, she sounded a lot better, and I didn't want to derail that by telling her exactly where I was calling from so I told a half-truth instead. "I'm on my way back from the gym. How are you feeling?"

"So much better," she assured me. "We can definitely skate today."

Between that news and the talk I'd just had with Amy, things were looking up all round. "Perfect. I'll see you in a little bit then."

From my reaction, Amy could guess how the conversation went, and as soon as I hung up, she grabbed my arm and pulled me up, pushing me towards the door. "Go and get ready. We'll talk tonight."

We definitely would, and on my way out the door, after a quick glance around the empty hallway to make sure no one could see, I gave her a quick kiss on the cheek before leaving. As soon as I got back to my room, I got back on my phone and made some plans for how we would spend our evening together, once everything was out in the open, my heart beating faster with anticipation than it ever had for any competition before.

The next few hours passed quickly, steeped in our usual pre-competition rituals, and soon, we were all waiting at the boards for our turn on the ice. Grace's recovery was a real stroke of luck. I could hardly believe how much better she looked, but then, her illness came on quickly too. Must have been one of those 24-hour things, and the timing certainly worked in our favour.

Now, we could get out there and show the whole world the amazing program that Amy had created. After all the drama and stress of the last few days, we could still end the weekend on a high.

"Knock 'em dead," Amy called out as we took the ice, an extra smile in her eyes just for me, and I smiled back at her, ignoring the look I could see Grace giving me from the corner of my eye.

The previous team must have skated well because the crowd cheered their marks, but I tuned it all out as much as I could. When our names were announced, Grace and I skated to the centre of the ice, acknowledging the crowd for the first time, and the arena fell silent as we took our starting positions.

The program was so new that we'd only performed it in full costume once before, but as soon as the first strains of the music filled the air around us, my heartbeat settled and my body took over.

It didn't matter that the program was new. Each step felt natural because it had been designed especially for us. In every movement, I could feel Amy right there beside me, even if Grace's body was the one in my grasp. Her voice whispered encouragement in my ear, the memory of her encouraging smile driving me on through the difficult footwork and lifts.

One lift in particular drew such a gasp from the crowd that I nearly broke character and smiled. The people in the audience were right there with us, fully invested, a give-and-take between us and them that was one of the very best parts of performing to a crowd.

When the music ended, I barely heard the cheering or Grace's excited squeal as we hugged. I didn't need to wait for the marks to know what just happened. We won; I felt it in my bones. The program felt easy and natural despite its difficulty, and we'd performed it almost flawlessly. The crowd were on their feet as Grace and I took our bows and Amy's face when we stepped off the ice confirmed my own belief about how well we'd done.

I pulled her and Brian along to sit in the kiss 'n' cry area with us to wait for our marks, and when they came up, they exceeded my expectations. A new personal best, the highest mark we'd ever received for a free dance, and as we watched the monitor, our names moved to the top of the leaderboard, just as I knew they would.

We won, securing our spot in the Grand Prix Final, and sending notice to all the other teams that if they wanted an Olympic medal that year, they were going to have to go through us.

Since we weren't at the point where I could throw my arms around Amy in public like I wanted to, I settled for giving her another quick kiss on the cheek. Hopefully, by the time we got to our next competition, I could show my appreciation for her properly.

I couldn't wait.

The usual flurry of reporters asked us questions backstage, giving me plenty of chances to praise Amy's program, and afterwards, we returned to the ice to receive our medals, followed by the rest of the post-competition requirements before we were able to change out of our costumes.

Finally, we were free to go back to the hotel on the athlete bus, our medals still hanging around our necks. Amy had made her own way back there again after whispering to me that she would be in her room, waiting for me.

All I had to do was break the news to Grace first.

"Let's go out somewhere to celebrate," Grace suggested as we got off the elevator on our floor. "One of the other skaters told me about this great club downtown..."

I cut her off before she could get carried away. "Actually, we need to talk. Let's go to your room for a minute."

A flash of excitement crossed her face at that suggestion, which wouldn't make what I had to tell her any easier, but I still had to say it, no matter what. The time for games was over.

She opened the door and walked in first while I followed, closing the door behind me. Before she could offer me a drink or a seat or anything else, I got right to the point. "I've already got plans for tonight. With Amy."

As I expected, Grace's face tightened, her nostrils flaring at the mention of Amy's name, but she tried to remain stoic. "I guess she could come too..."

Again, I didn't let her finish. "No, Grace. Amy and I are going out *alone*. On a date. We're going to be seeing each other now, publicly. I wanted you to be the first to know."

The mask of stoicism fell away in an instant, replaced by a pained look of hurt and maybe even betrayal. "You said you weren't dating her. "When you brought her on, we talked about it, and you said..."

"I remember what I said, and I wasn't dating her then. Now, I will be. It doesn't change anything for us on the ice, Grace. We're still a team and I'm still completely focused on our season. This is only about my personal life, it doesn't change anything between us."

I knew that was only partly true. It might not change anything for me, but she'd always held onto a hope of something more between us, no matter how clear I tried to be that it would never happen.

"But... the judges," she protested, falling back on the same excuses everyone always used. "The fans, they all think..."

"What they all think is wrong. We were never together and you know that."

She flinched, but I pressed on, focusing back on the potential impact for our skating and away from her hurt feelings as much as possible.

"You saw the marks we got today. Even if we take a bit of a hit when they realize we're not a couple, which would be ridiculous, by the way, we've got enough of a buffer that it doesn't matter."

"The Olympics are only three months away," she tried next. "Is it really worth it to do this right now? Why can't you just wait..."

"It's worth it to me," I interrupted once again. I didn't have a single doubt about that, and I didn't want to debate it with her any more than I already had. "This is what I want. It's what I've wanted for longer than I care to admit, and this time, nothing is going to stand in my way."

Chapter Seven

~Amelia~

Still buzzing with the excitement of Austin and Grace's win, I barely had a chance to step inside my room at the hotel before Austin knocked at my door. My stomach flipped when I opened it and found him standing there with a wide grin on his face, his eyes bright, and no sign of the tension of the last few days anywhere to be seen.

With a bob of his head, he gestured to the elevator at the end of the hall, his dark hair flopping over his forehead with the movement. "Come on. We're going to celebrate."

The fluttering in my stomach intensified, anticipation joining the excitement already bubbling there. Were we celebrating his win, or more than that?

"Did you talk to Grace?"

I blurted the question out, bracing myself for a 'no' answer. Something always seemed to stop things from coming together for us, but to my great relief, Austin nodded.

"I did. She knows the truth now, so let's get out of here before anyone else tries to stop us."

He'd obviously noticed our unfortunate habit of being interrupted as much as I did, and I let out a shaky laugh as my heart swelled with hope.

"Do I need to change?" I glanced down at the sweater and jeans I'd worn to the rink, perfect for keeping warm rink-side but not appropriate for a fancy restaurant or club. I had no idea what he had in mind.

His smile somehow grew even wider. "Trust me, it really doesn't matter what you wear. Let's just go. *Please*."

The desperation in his voice drew another breathy laugh from me, and I grabbed my bag, my hands shaking as I double-checked I had my room key before closing the door behind me and following Austin out of the hotel.

As soon as we were outside, Austin's hand found mine, his thumb rubbing along the back of my hand in a way that sent shivers through me despite the heat of his skin against mine. He'd held my hands a million times on the ice, but never off of it.

It felt different, in the very best way.

"Is this okay?" he asked softly, his fingers intertwining with mine in a firm, possessive gesture that sent the butterflies in my stomach soaring. No one else's touch had ever had that kind of effect on me.

"It's perfect. You don't care if anyone sees us?"

After the photos in the restaurant the other day, he had to know what would happen if we were spotted, but his hand squeezed mine, lending extra weight to his words. "I'm not worried about anybody right now but you and me. We're done hiding."

Relief washed over me, followed by a tidal wave of happiness so strong, I couldn't think of anything to say to adequately express it. Luckily, he didn't seem to mind. We walked in comfortable silence for a couple of minutes, simply enjoying the feeling of being together and savouring our newfound freedom.

"Where are we going?" I asked eventually, realizing that I still didn't know.

"To another hotel."

I nearly stumbled over my own feet in surprise. "Wh-what?"

He said it as though going to a hotel together, aside from the one we were officially staying at for business, was a perfectly normal thing to do, but when I stuttered out my response, his cheeks turned an adorable shade of pink beneath the streetlights as he realized exactly what his suggestion sounded like. "No, that's not what I... I didn't mean... it's not to get a room."

He muttered a curse under his breath that made me smile. It seemed I wasn't the only one feeling a little nervous about the new state of our relationship.

"A hotel a few blocks away has a spa with a private onsen. Open-air hot springs. After the weekend we've had, I thought we could have a nice, relaxing evening with no one else around."

That sounded perfect, and very thoughtful of him. And it wasn't that I didn't want to be alone in a hotel room with Austin; eventually, I hoped that would be normal for us. I just didn't expect it to happen on our very first official date.

Thankfully, he didn't seem to expect it either. The alternative he'd come up with to get us some time alone sounded wonderful, except for one obvious flaw. "I don't have a bathing suit with me."

"Actually, it's traditional in Japan not to wear anything."

I didn't stumble that time, but my cheeks warmed against the cool air as I tried to decide if he was being serious. Getting into a hot spring together naked seemed like a pretty big leap for a first date, but Austin only laughed when he noticed my blush.

"It'll be fine. The water's cloudy and it's night time, so there won't be much to see. I promise it won't be weird."

Yeah, right. Having a naked Austin a few feet away from me after pining over him for years would be perfectly normal. Even in my head it sounded sarcastic.

"I'm beginning to think I don't really know you at all," I said, only half-joking.

"You do," he promised. "And you trust me enough to give this a try, right?"

I couldn't argue with that.

When we arrived at the hotel, Austin and I were shown to separate changing rooms to get undressed. The changing rooms were private, just like the onsen, so nobody could see the way my hands shook as I pulled off my sweater and unbuttoned my jeans, sliding them down with a shiver that had far more to do with nerves than the temperature.

Large, fluffy towels sat on a small table by the door that led to the onsen, and I wrapped one around myself before stepping out onto the deck, my heart pounding so loud, it felt like a drummer sitting in my ear.

The square-shaped hot-spring pool shimmered in the low lighting of the lanterns that lined the deck. Above the water, I could just make out a few twinkling stars in the night sky, along with a mellow glow of lights from the city around us. As Austin promised, the darkness hid a great deal, and it wasn't until I got close to the rock edges of the pool that I could make out the muscles of Austin's shoulders and arms, spread out to either side of him as he stretched out on one side of the pool.

I'd seen naked men before. Four long years had passed since I got my first kiss from Ben on another winter's night, and I'd had boyfriends in that time. I'd slept with two of them, and it had been fine, if not particularly earth-shattering.

But the man in the water wasn't just *any* man.

He'd been my partner, my dream, and the guy who broke my heart without meaning to. The one I thought I'd never get a chance with, and now, he sat naked in the water in front of me, waiting for me to join him to kick off our first official date.

Neither my heart nor my brain could fully process it, so I did my best to take in the moment without the weight of our past or the promise of the future. Later, I could work through exactly what it all meant to me; for now, I simply wanted to enjoy it.

As I stepped into Austin's line of vision, he turned to look at me, and my stomach flipped again with a glimpse of the enticing, dimpled smile I had always loved.

His eyes travelled down my body wrapped tightly in the towel, until they got to my legs. His smile instantly fell away.

"Is that from your accident?"

I didn't have to look to know he meant the long, slightly indented red line that ran all the way down the outside of my calf on my right leg. The surgery that reconstructed my broken bones had been a complete success, but the scar remained, as the doctor warned me it would.

"It is. Believe it or not, it looks a lot better than it used to."

His mouth twisted into a grimace. "Does it still hurt?"

"No, not at all."

His eyes returned to my face and, even in the darkness, I could make out the lingering sadness in them. "I'm so sorry you had to go through any of that."

"I know," I assured him. I might have gone through more physical pain than he did but we'd both paid the emotional price and I didn't want to dwell on it. "Can we not talk about any of that tonight?"

He nodded, understanding me immediately. "No looking back."

"Exactly." I gave him a smile before looking over at the steps down into the water, calculating my next move. "I'm ready to get in, but you have to close your eyes."

His warm chuckle convinced me even more than his words did that he wanted to move on too. "Of course. I promise I won't peek."

Leaning back, he rested his head on the edge of the pool and shut his eyes. With a deep breath, I threw the towel next to the pool and slipped into the water, sitting on the opposite side of the pool from Austin.

Looking down at myself, I could make out the vague shape of my body but nothing more than that. When I chanced a glance over at Austin, I couldn't see any of him beneath the water's cloudy surface either. He'd been telling the truth, and I relaxed even more as the warm water soaked into my skin.

"Okay, I'm in."

His head raised and his smile returned as he saw me there, as if he'd been afraid I might disappear when his eyes were closed.

I knew the feeling; I could hardly believe we were actually there either.

Since he'd been so busy after he and Grace got off the ice, we hadn't had a chance to talk about the competition yet. I figured that would be a safe enough topic to start with now that we were settled.

"You must be pretty happy about your win."

The light of the poolside lanterns reflected off his eyes, making them twinkle. "The program is amazing. It's going to make all the difference for us. If we skate like that at the Olympics, I really think we can win."

Honestly, I thought so too, but I might have been biased, considering I choreographed the program and my favourite skater performed it.

We talked a bit more about the training he would need to do before the Games. He and Grace had the Grand Prix final the next month and the Canadian championships in January before heading to the Olympics in February. Meanwhile, my work with them had pretty much come to an end. I might need to go to the rink once or twice to check that everything still looked crisp and tight, but otherwise, when we got back to Toronto, I needed to rededicate myself to school and my internship.

Dating would be a little tricky with our conflicting schedules, but as he smiled at me across the water, I didn't have any doubt it would be worth the effort to make it work.

Every minute spent with him would be worth it.

Gradually, the conversation turned more personal and Austin brought up my dating history in a roundabout way.

"Any jealous exes I need to be aware of?"

His tone teased, but I could feel the genuine curiosity behind the question.

"I've dated a bit, but it's never been too serious. Nobody's still hanging around, so you don't have to worry about that." When he seemed satisfied with that, I turned the question back on him. "What about you? You must have dated a few other people?"

His steady stream of dates when we skated together had always made me jealous, but to my surprise, he shook his head. "Not really. I mean, I've been on dates, but nothing I'd call a relationship. It's hard to connect with someone when skating is my life and I'm sort-of pretending to date someone else."

That actually made sense once I thought about it. In the last few years, whenever I heard about him, Grace was the only woman mentioned.

"Besides, there hasn't been anyone who's really made my heart race in a long time."

Although I knew exactly what he meant from the way my own heart seemed determined to set a new speed record that night, I tried to play it cool. "And that's what you're looking for?"

His dimple made another appearance and my stomach fluttered. "That's what I'm looking *at*."

"Austin." His name came out sounding strangled and unnatural with my heart lodged in my throat and his eyes laser-focused on me. The intensity of my feelings and all the uncertainty that came with them was almost too much to take, but alone with him, both of us naked beneath the water, I had nowhere to hide.

No choice but to face it head-on.

"You don't believe me?" He slipped off his seat and moved towards me, sending my heart rate spiking even higher. "Give me your hand."

Before I could question it, my hand extended. He caught it tenderly in his and pulled it towards himself, drawing even closer to me. My palm connected with his firm, muscular chest, and I felt it: the insistent drumming of his heart, the same way it felt after we skated a four-and-a-half-minute program, the adrenaline of the performance and the crowd rushing through us.

Except now, it beat that way because of me.

He leaned towards me until his eyes were all I could see. "It's always beaten for you."

I couldn't say whether he moved the final few inches or if I moved towards him, but in the next instant, our lips were connected and the rest of the world fell away.

The fact that we were naked? Forgotten. The foreign country around us, the competition, the fans, everything about the past few days faded into the background. Nothing remained but the soft firmness of his lips, the scent of his cologne, and the way my whole body responded to him, as if pure electricity passed from his mouth to mine.

His free hand, the one not still holding mine against his chest, reached up to caress my face as he deepened the kiss, his tongue pushing gently against my lips until they gave way to him. His tongue brushed against mine, sending a shiver down my spine despite the warm water enveloping me. He tasted familiar, as if all those times kissing him in my dreams had been real, and entirely new at the same time. If our first kiss had burned itself into my memory, this one seared itself across my heart.

When he finally pulled away, all the air left my lungs along with him. I couldn't seem to catch my breath.

He stroked my cheek once again with his hand before moving back far enough that his breath no longer skated across my skin. The smile on his face held the same wonder and satisfaction that I felt down to my soul. "That was even better than I remembered it."

"Then why are you stopping?" I demanded breathlessly.

He exhaled a tight laugh. "They have rules here about getting too... uh, intimate... in the pool. I'm going to go sit back down before we get in any trouble."

From the awkward way he shuffled over to the other side of the pool, I didn't have to wonder if the kiss affected him the same way it did for me, and I couldn't help the giggle that slipped out at his predicament. The dirty look he threw me did nothing to lessen my amusement, and when I laughed harder, he began to chuckle too.

Being able to laugh with him and tease him that way, with none of the other background noise of our life interfering, left me feeling lighter than I had in days. In years, even, and I knew exactly where that lightness came from.

Hope.

Austin felt it too, as his next question made clear. "So, what do you think? Are we giving this a proper try? Are we officially a couple now?"

I couldn't have held back my beaming smile even if I wanted to. "Yeah. I think we are."

He reached out again to grab my hand and kiss it before immediately moving back again, as if he needed to keep the space between us to resist any further temptation.

We talked a while longer, about everything and nothing, until the time came to get out. Austin went first, and despite my very strong desire to peek as he got out of the pool, I managed to keep my eyes from wandering. Once we changed back into our clothes, we headed back onto the street, towards our hotel, walking hand in hand once again.

He hadn't said anything about his plans for the rest of the evening, but if he didn't ask me to his room, I would ask him to mine. We'd had enough foreplay. Years of wanting and wishing, and I didn't want to wait any longer.

Austin Black was finally my boyfriend, and this time, nothing could stand in our way.

~**Austin**~

I'd had a lot of memorable moments in my life: national championships and world medals, fans cheering my name and front-page stories in the newspapers, but I couldn't remember ever feeling as good as I did walking back to the hotel with Amy's hand in mine. The evening together went exactly as I hoped it would. After all the wasted time, we were both completely on the same page with nothing holding us back, both ready to take the next step.

I wanted to tell everyone we passed on the street that the amazing woman next to me had agreed to be mine.

I wanted the whole world to know.

First up would be Brian, and I explained my logic to Amy as we arrived back at the hotel. "I think we should go talk to Brian while we've got a chance to speak to him alone, before we all go to the airport in the morning. I'll let him know that we're going to be seeing each other and that Grace is aware of it and might be a little put out for a while. He should get a heads up about that."

"I'll follow your lead," she promised, giving my hand an extra-tight squeeze.

The evening had turned into night by the time we reached his room, but normally, my coach was a bit of a night owl, especially with the adrenaline of a competition day, so I didn't worry too much about disturbing him when I knocked on his door.

I certainly didn't expect to see his room full of people when he opened the door, though.

Grace and her parents sat on the bed, my mother stood on the far side of the room, while Kevin sat to the side, his face as somber as Brian's at the door. What the hell did we miss?

"You got my message?" Brian asked.

Focused entirely on Amy, I'd forgotten to turn my phone back on when I got dressed again after the onsen. Only when he asked did I realize I hadn't looked at it in a couple of hours. "No, actually. Were you trying to reach me?"

He exhaled deeply. "For the last hour. Come in, both of you."

I glanced down at Amy, who shrugged her shoulders in reply, confirming she had no idea what any of this meant either. It couldn't be because of my conversation with Grace, could it? She'd been upset, sure, but involving our entire team seemed like a pretty severe overreaction.

As we stepped into the room, it didn't take me long to pick up that things were even more serious than I'd initially suspected. Tears stood in Grace's eyes, with traces of them streaking down her face, and everyone else looked like they were in shock. No colour remained in my mom's face and Brian didn't look much better.

This had to be about more than just my relationship status. My heart pounded as I looked from face-to-face, trying to get some clue. Honestly, it looked like someone had died, but with all the people closest to me in the world there in that room, that didn't fully make sense either.

"What happened?" I finally asked when no one spoke. I barely noticed Amy's hand hadn't left mine until she squeezed it again in support.

Brian broke the silence, taking a deep breath before he spoke. "We've been contacted by the International Skating Union. They've disqualified you from this event."

Grace's tears came faster as she buried her face in her hands, her shoulders shaking with silent sobs.

"Disqualified?" I repeated incredulously. That couldn't be right. We'd never been disqualified before and we hadn't done anything wrong.

Brian nodded grimly, confirming that I'd heard him correctly. "For a doping violation."

Doping?

We were talking about *drugs*? That made even less sense than being disqualified over a technicality. Performance-enhancing drugs didn't even work in our sport; no drugs could improve skating quality. And even if they existed, we certainly didn't take any.

"It has to be a mistake." My voice came out flat, my body feeling strangely numb. This couldn't be real. "Can we re-do the test?"

Brian's eyes flicked over to Grace before coming back to me. "It's not a mistake, Austin. At least, the results aren't a mistake. Grace told us everything. Although unintentional, she took something for her illness that she didn't clear with the team doctor. The test is correct."

My mouth fell open as ice-cold shock rushed through me, numbing me even further.

"I'm sorry," Grace managed to sob before breaking down completely. Her mom quickly embraced her, pulling Grace tight to her chest, and with the sound of her voice, the wall of detachment around me cracked.

Anger roared in first, anger both at the situation and at Grace in particular. How could she have been so careless? From our first day on the national team, the coaching staff drilled into our heads that every single medication we took, even over-the-counter meds, had to be cleared with the team doctor first, for this exact reason. She knew that just as well as I did.

"What did you take?"

Despite feeling like my world had tilted and begun to spin out of control, I tried to keep my voice level. Even so, Grace's sobs wouldn't let her answer me, so Brian did it for her.

"Apparently, one of the other skaters heard she was sick and gave her something. Grace thought if it had been cleared by *their* team's doctor, it must be okay."

"I just... wanted... to skate... today," Grace whimpered through her tears, which only fed my fury.

That was no excuse. I *told* her we could withdraw if she didn't feel up to it. She made the choice to compete no matter the cost, and now, we were paying the price.

"Why did it matter so much?" I whispered, because keeping my voice down was the only way I could stop myself from yelling. Exploding at her wouldn't do any good when the damage had already been done, but I needed answers.

Grace's eyes went to my hand, still joined with Amy's, before flicking over to my mom. My stomach sank as I followed her gaze. Why did my mom always seem to be in the middle of everything?

"Don't give me that look," my mom said, her face still pale but her voice as defiant as ever as she glared back at Grace. "I never told you to self-medicate. I thought you'd have a little more sense than that."

"Cynthia," Brian warned as Grace's parents both sputtered at my mom in outrage. "Let's keep this civil. We're all upset."

"You told me I had to skate!" Grace cried, the words aimed at my mom. "You said if I didn't, Mia would win."

My control snapped and my words came out as a roar as I also addressed my mother. "Win what? Another of your ridiculous games that we didn't even know we were playing? The only thing any of us came here to win was this competition!"

My mom looked every one of her forty-seven years as her lips pulled tight, her glare directed at Amy. "If that's all she came here for, why did she spend all night with that reporter at the bar, kissing him so he'd write his ridiculous story making her sound like some kind of saint?"

I could barely process all of that. By 'reporter', she must have meant Ben, but what bar? What kissing?

"Did you have me followed?" Amy's voice quivered in anger that mirrored my own. "Austin fired you, so you decided to spy on me to try to change his mind?"

The most ridiculous thing about the accusation was that it could easily have been true. I still didn't know what Amy kissing Ben had to do with anything, especially since she hadn't denied it, but I pushed that aside to focus on the one thing I had never understood when it came to my mother, something I was determined to get to the bottom of, once and for all.

"Why do you hate Amy so much? What did she ever do to you?" I pulled my new girlfriend closer to my side as I spoke, wanting to shield her from whatever ridiculous answer my mom had, but also wanting her to hear it too. She deserved to know the answer just as much as I did.

Bitterness filled my mom's eyes as she answered. "Everyone thinks she's so special. She has to be the centre of attention, all the time, and your attention especially. When you first started skating together, I heard 'Amy this' and 'Amy that', all day long. You were never like that with Grace."

Grace let out another whimpered sob in the background and my eyes closed in frustration. Tact and my mother had never been very well acquainted.

"When she left, I finally got you back again," my mom continued. "Until she turned up again and you went right back to falling all over yourself for her. Now, the media is on her side, talking about how she's so inspirational, and it's too much, Austin! It has to end."

It had to end, all right, but not in the way she meant. Finally, I had the truth: it really just came down to jealousy. My mom thought I liked Amy more than I liked her, and at that particular moment, I couldn't argue with her.

I opened my mouth to respond, but before I could, Amy stepped in, her focus moving away from my mother and back to Brian.

"I think we're all getting off topic. You said they've been disqualified from this event, but you haven't told us yet what this means for the rest of the season."

As soon as the words were out of her mouth, the ground shifted beneath me again. I had been so focused on the immediate consequences, losing our result in this event and the reputational hit that would come with it, that I hadn't thought any further ahead yet.

I didn't know all the rules around doping since I never thought I'd have to, but I did know they were very strict about it. Amy's words made me realize that disqualifying us from this one event wouldn't be the end of it.

Everyone else in the room exchanged devastated glances, Grace's sobs became even more intense, and I had a sinking feeling that I knew what the answer would be before Brian said the words.

He directed his answer at me even though Amy had been the one to ask it. "The season's over. You've been suspended for a year. I'm so sorry, Austin, but you're not going to the Olympics this year after all."

Chapter Eight

~Amelia~

My heart cracked as Austin's dream crumbled in front of me.

I knew what it felt like to have my future taken away from me through no fault of my own, so I had some idea how he felt at that moment, but on the other hand, I hadn't been as close to achieving my dream as he had been. In a matter of months, he could have had an Olympic medal around his neck, and with Brian's words, that possibility vanished right in front of him, evaporating into thin air.

His hand went slack in mine, all the energy drained from his body.

"Why, Grace?" he whispered, looking back over at her with none of the anger I'd seen in his face earlier. Now, I could only see despair. "I still don't understand. What would have possibly been worth this?"

Grace grabbed a tissue from the box in her mom's hands and blew her nose loudly. "I just wanted you to appreciate me. I've worked just as hard for this as you have."

His exhale dripped with frustration. "Of course you have. I never said otherwise."

I believed that without question. Austin never belittled his partner's contribution, not mine and not Grace's.

"But I was never good enough for you," Grace countered, her face contorting in her own pain and grief. "Not compared to *her*."

The disgust in that word as she looked over at me sent a shudder down my spine, and Austin pulled me closer to him, as if to protect me. The simple gesture filled me with warmth that helped to dispel some of the chill from Grace's words.

"You left me for her in the first place, and after her accident, when I dropped everything to skate with you again, you made it clear that it would only be temporary until she got better."

Wait, *what*? Austin left her to skate with me? I knew he had a partner before me but he never once mentioned it had been Grace. Why didn't he tell me?

As much as I wanted to know, I bit my tongue since Grace still had more to say. In fact, now that she'd started, she didn't seem to be able to stop as years of frustration poured out of her.

"She didn't even try to get in touch with you again after you never called her new number. I wouldn't have given up like that. I would have fought for you. Why couldn't you ever see that?"

Ice rushed through my veins and Austin stiffened next to me. He'd obviously noticed the same thing I did: the mention of my 'new number', the one I got after my accident. The one Austin never got. How did Grace know anything about that?

Her face paled as she realized what she'd said, and she looked down, avoiding his gaze as Austin's stony glare landed on her. "What do you know about Amy's new phone number?"

My eyes darted to Mrs Black to see if she knew about this, but she looked as surprised as anyone else. She didn't normally hide her feelings well, so I believed her surprise was genuine.

Grace must have decided she had nothing left to lose because she blurted out something close to the truth. "Karen wrote it down for you one day at the rink but you were having a shower or something. I told her I'd give it to you, but I... I lost it."

The last part, I didn't buy for a second. It seemed much more likely she'd 'lost it' on purpose, but the rest of what she said rang true. Finally, the last piece of the puzzle fell into place.

Grace made sure Austin never got my number. My mom had told me the truth about that, at least: she really did give Karen my new number to give to Austin, and Karen tried to pass it on. We just hadn't counted on Austin's jealous partner intercepting it along the way.

The tension in Austin's body hadn't loosened at all, so I gave his hand another squeeze, trying to show my support.

He took a deep breath before squeezing it back and addressing Grace in a flat, cool voice devoid of any emotion. It sounded worse than if he'd yelled. "It still doesn't explain what you were thinking, taking that medication. How could you think that was okay?"

"The other skater told Grace the medication was safe," Grace's mom said, jumping in for the first time to stick up for her daughter. "That girl could have done this on purpose. Maybe she was trying to sabotage them."

"Maybe," Brian agreed diplomatically, also stepping back in now that we were back to talking about Austin and Grace's career instead of their relationship. "But even if that were the case, and even if we could prove it, it doesn't matter. Grace still took the medication and the ISU has a zero-tolerance policy. We can't fight it. I've already spoken to them for over an hour. There's nothing we can do."

"There has to be *something*," Mrs Black spoke up. "We can appeal it somehow."

Her voice almost always grated on my nerves, but at that moment, I only heard the devastation in her tone. Austin's career had been her dream too, no matter how overbearing she could be about it, and all of her hopes had just been crushed too.

"There really isn't, Cynthia," Brian said, sounding weary and sad. "I've looked at every possibility. Grace can't compete in any ISU competition for the next year."

"*Grace* can't," Mrs Black repeated. "That doesn't mean Austin can't."

Everyone in the room gaped at her in surprise, even me. I thought I'd seen the depths of her tactlessness, but apparently, she could go even lower.

"I don't think this is the time..." Brian tried to say, while Grace's parents both shouted at her in outrage.

"You are the most inconsiderate..."

"Do you ever think about anyone else..."

The room devolved into a shouting match while Grace began crying again.

"I need to get out of here," Austin whispered in my ear, cutting through all the commotion. The second I nodded in agreement, he pulled me from the room without a word to anyone. My hand still held in his, Austin led me to his room and closed the door behind us.

"I'm so sorry," I said as soon as we were alone, though I knew perhaps better than anyone how inadequate those words were. "Do you want anything? We could go for a walk, or get a drink, or I could give you some time alone..."

"No." His voice sounded weak, his shoulders slumped in defeat. "Please, don't leave me alone."

Instantly, my arms wrapped around him. "I won't. I'm here, Austin. I wish there was more I could do, but I'm here for you."

He returned my embrace, his chin resting on top of my head as he held me tight to his chest. I inhaled his familiar scent, muted by the waters of the onsen but still undeniably him.

"Did you really kiss Ben?" he asked after a moment, and in spite of everything, I almost laughed. With the world falling apart around him, he was worried about *that*?

"He kissed me." Austin's arms tensed around me, and I quickly continued. "For like half a second, because I wouldn't admit that I liked you.

When I didn't kiss him back, he figured out the truth. That's all. It didn't mean anything."

A sigh slipped through his lips and his muscles relaxed but he still didn't let me go.

"Why didn't you ever tell me Grace was your first partner?" If we were going to avoid talking about the bigger issue, I might as well get my question answered too.

"It didn't seem important at the time since you didn't even know Grace, and since you came back, there hasn't been an appropriate time to bring it up. I didn't want to rock the boat if I didn't have to. But it's true: I skated with Grace first, which is why my mom brought her in when you got hurt."

We stood in silence for a moment longer, floating between the past and present, all the secrets and all the misunderstandings and everything that had led us to that moment.

"It's like I'm cursed," Austin whispered, his words barely audible. "Things keep happening to my partners."

The two situations were nothing alike, other than that they both affected him, and I didn't want him to feel that way. "This isn't your fault, and neither was my accident. You didn't do anything wrong."

He let out a grunt of acknowledgement that didn't necessarily sound like agreement. "I just can't believe this, Amy. I can't believe this is how it ends."

I pulled out of his embrace far enough that I could look him in the eyes. "This isn't the end. It's only for a year. Yes, it's an Olympic year, and that really, really sucks, but trust me, life does go on. You guys will keep training even if you're not competing, and you'll come back better than ever..."

I had more to say, but Austin shook his head at me, his face cloaked in sadness. "I'd already pretty much decided this would be my last competitive year. I don't want to go for another four years, and after everything she just said, I really don't want to skate with Grace again at all."

He'd never mentioned wanting to quit before, so I had to assume the shock of the situation was to blame. "You don't need to decide anything right now. We'll go back to Toronto, put a week or two under your belt and I'm sure you'll feel differently."

He released me fully and took a step back, rubbing his hands over his face. When he lowered them, a new expression settled on his face, one I couldn't quite place.

"There is one other option: the one my mom brought up. Not that I agree with her timing in suggesting it, but she did have a point."

My forehead creased as I tried to follow his train of thought. His mom said that the suspension only applied to Grace and not to Austin, but how could he skate without a partner...?

A second later, it hit me, and my brow cleared, my eyes going wide instead.

"You can't be serious."

He couldn't actually be suggesting that I could take Grace's place? There were too many reasons why it wouldn't work and I refused to let my hopes even get off the ground. I couldn't let my heart be broken that way all over again.

The determination in his eyes grew firmer. "You know all the programs. Hell, you even created one of them. We already have the same basic technique. It wouldn't be like starting from scratch like it would be with anyone else."

"I haven't trained properly in four years," I countered, just as firmly. "My conditioning is nowhere near where it would need to be. The Games are only three months away."

My protests did nothing to deter him. "So we train every day. We train harder than we've ever trained before. I'll be right by your side, the whole way."

Even if I *could* get back into shape in time, there were other obstacles to consider. "Would Skate Canada even allow it? I don't have any senior international skating credits."

Somehow, he already knew the answer to that. "We would need to come first or second at the Canadian championships, and even if we didn't, I think they would give us some leeway. We can talk to them about it. They won't want to lose their medal chance any more than I do."

"Austin..." I tried to protest again, but my conviction had begun to waver and Austin sensed it, not letting me make any other excuses as he took my hands in his.

"Neither of us planned it, but we might have just been given a second chance. This time, I'm not letting you go without a fight. We can do this."

I opened my mouth, but any words I meant to say died in my throat as I let myself picture it for the first time. Training with Austin, competing with him, working towards the dream that we'd built together all those years ago.

Could it actually come true?

"Please, Amy," he whispered, a look of such tenderness and hopefulness on his face that my heart melted into a puddle inside my chest. "Dance with me."

~Austin~

I could see the battle going on in Amy's head reflected in her eyes as she stared up at me with a wide-eyed, dazed expression. I knew she wanted this. The chance for us to skate together again, to work towards the Olympics as we always should have done, we *both* wanted it, but fear held her back. Fear of getting her hopes up only to have it all pulled out from beneath her again.

I understood it, but I also knew she couldn't let that fear rule her life. The girl I fell for all those years ago would never have let fear stop her, and if I accomplished nothing else that evening, I wanted to help her to find that girl inside herself again.

"Do you remember what you said to me the first time we skated together?" I asked, still holding her hands in mine.

Her cheeks flushed as her eyes dropped to our joined hands. "I was only thirteen years old."

"Exactly. And what did you say?"

Tentatively, her blue eyes returned to my face, her cheeks still pink. "I told you I was going to win a gold medal at the Olympics."

"And?" I prompted.

Her mouth twitched into something close to a smile. "And that if you wanted to be the one beside me when I did, you better be ready to work hard."

I remembered that day as clearly as if it were yesterday. The confidence radiating out of that girl whenever she took the ice inspired me that day, and every day after. That explained why I still kept her picture in my locker, all those years later.

"I did work hard, and so did you, and that medal is still there for the taking. We can still get it if you take this leap with me. As long as you're still ready to work hard, I am too."

I could see in her face how close she was to agreeing, but something still held her back. I had no idea what it might be until she laid it out for me. "What about Grace? She'll be really hurt. I know how it felt when you chose to skate with someone else."

That reminder of the pain I caused Amy made me wince. I didn't want to hurt Grace either, but it had nothing to do with her anymore as far as I could tell.

"We wouldn't even be talking about this if it weren't for the choices that Grace made, and we would only be skating together for this season, during her suspension. I know she didn't mean for this to happen, but there's nothing anyone can do to change it now. Isn't that what you've been telling me? We can't spend our time worrying about the 'what ifs'. This is the card we've been dealt. This is the only thing we can control, and the only choice we have to make right now."

I pulled her closer to me so we were nearly nose-to-nose, our eyes locked on each other.

"You're allowed to want this, Amy. You're allowed to have this dream. I want to do this for you too, not just for me. You're the best dancer I've ever known and you deserve to have this chance. All you have to decide right now is: do you want to dance with me again? Yes or no?"

Her eyes searched mine for a long moment, my heart thudding heavily with each passing second, but when her lips began to curl into a smile, I knew what her answer would be before she whispered the word.

"Yes."

As soon as she said it, my mouth found hers, sealing her agreement with a kiss. Her lips against mine felt like a promise for the future and the fulfillment of a dream all at the same time.

It should have been impossible, but somehow, after all the years apart, we were back together in every way that mattered. She'd already agreed to be my girlfriend and now, we were going to skate together too.

Logically, I should have probably been more upset. I should have felt badly for Grace, and part of me did, but I couldn't help the excitement that bubbled up inside me at the same time. Skating with Amy had always made me happier than anything, and I didn't intend to apologize for being happy that I'd have the chance to finish what we started the way we always should have.

"We should go and talk to Brian," I suggested as I pulled away from her. "We'll need to talk to someone at Skate Canada to get things started, and..."

Amy placed a finger over my lips, shaking her head gently. "Not tonight. Everyone's already dealing with a lot. Let's talk about it with him in the morning."

She had a point; I was getting ahead of myself, but I couldn't help it. "What will you do about school? I guess you'll have to take time off, we'll need all the time for training..."

"Austin," she cut me off again with a laugh. "I don't know yet. We literally decided five seconds ago. We'll figure it out tomorrow, okay?"

Knowing she was right, I shut my mouth and held her tighter in my arms. "I'm sorry. I'm just excited."

"I am too, but I think I need to sleep on it. Maybe when I wake up, I'll be more convinced that it's not just a dream."

Sleep didn't seem to be on the cards, but I could definitely get behind the idea of going to bed. With that in mind, I bent down to kiss her again, but to my surprise, she took a step back, out of my reach.

"I'm going to head back to my room now."

My eyebrows drew together in confusion. Maybe I needed to be clearer about what I wanted? We didn't need any further misunderstandings. "You can sleep here with me. I'd like you to stay."

Her eyes closed for a second, a soft exhale leaving her lips before she looked back up at me with an apologetic smile. "I don't know if that's a good idea."

Disappointment spiked in my chest, along with a deepening confusion. After what happened in the onsen, I thought we were on the same page, as ready as each other to move our relationship to the next level, but maybe her mood had shifted with everything else that just happened.

Not wanting her to feel any pressure, I elaborated further. "We don't have to do anything you're not ready for. If you want to just go to sleep, that's fine, but at least this way, when we wake up and see each other, we'll know for sure that we didn't dream it."

Her sweet smile eased some of my concern but not all of it, especially when she took another step back. "It's not that I'm not ready or that I don't want to. I just think that if we're really doing this, if we're going to skate together again, we might need to put the dating side of things on hold."

I could only blink at her, the words refusing to sink in. "Why?"

"You know why. The reason we waited until now to even talk about dating is because we knew it could complicate our working relationship. That's an even bigger risk now. We'll need every minute of training time we can get and we can't afford to let ourselves be distracted."

Despite the sense in what she said, I still couldn't stop myself from arguing with her. "It doesn't have to be one or the other, Amy. We can have both a relationship *and* a partnership. It's possible."

"Maybe it will be eventually, but I don't think that time is now. Trust me, I'm not saying this because I don't want to be with you. You know that's not true. The idea of waiting is as frustrating for me as it is for you, but we have to be practical about this."

Her face tightened as the next words came out of her mouth.

"The last time you kissed me while we were skating together, it didn't end well."

I groaned, not because she didn't have a point, but because she did. "Amy, nothing like that is going to happen again. This time, we'll talk things out properly. If something upsets one of us, we'll talk it through. We've grown up a lot since then."

"But why take the risk?" she asked softly. "It's better if nothing upsets us in the first place."

My hands scrubbed my face again, my frustration mingling with a kind of grim satisfaction. I had just been thinking that I wanted my no-nonsense Amy back and it looked like I had her, both the good and the bad sides that came with that.

I tried to provoke her, to push her buttons to draw out some emotion instead of cool logic. "Are you really breaking up with me an hour after you agreed to date me?"

She refused to take the bait, answering me calmly. "I'm not breaking up with you, I'm just saying we should press the pause button for a while. Neither of us is going to date anyone else. If we're training as hard as we need to, there won't be time."

She had that right.

"So, let's just focus on skating for now. After the Games, we can pick up where we left off."

After the Games. Three months felt like a lifetime when we'd been so close to finally moving forward, but if I listened to my brain instead of other parts of my body, I could see she had a point. If we were going to make a proper run at qualifying for the Games, there wouldn't be time for distractions. We really would need every second we had.

"Let's sleep on it," she suggested. "*Separately.* We can see how we feel in the morning."

With no intention of forcing her into a situation that made her uncomfortable, I had little choice but to agree, giving her a soft kiss goodnight before she headed back to her room.

Sleep didn't come easily with all the thoughts running through my head, but eventually, morning arrived and I knocked on Amy's door as soon as I thought she'd be up. She opened the door already dressed and ready to go.

"Let's go talk to Brian," she said as soon as she saw me, and a smile spread across my face. I recognized this version of Amy, the one who knew exactly what she wanted and would do everything in her power to get it.

A few minutes later, we sat across from our coach and his husband in their room while we laid out our proposal for the coming months. Brian's gaze flickered between Amy and I, sober and serious but far less surprised than I expected him to look.

"I hoped you would come to this conclusion. I would have suggested it myself if you hadn't, I just didn't think last night was the right time."

"So, you think it will work?" Amy asked. "Can I compete?"

"You can compete at the Canadian championships, I'm certain. I'll pull some strings at Skate Canada if I have to, but I don't think it'll be a problem. As to whether you can compete at the Olympics, that will depend on how things go at Canadians."

Amy and I exchanged glances, both of us nodding in understanding. We expected as much.

"It's going to be tough," Brian added, which we'd already acknowledged between us as well. "There are only two months until Canadians, three until the Olympics. You obviously know the choreography, Mia, but knowing it and skating it are two different things."

"She'll be ready," I promised. "If you'll train us, we can do it."

At last, he cracked a small smile. "Well, then, I guess we better get to work."

Chapter Nine

~Amelia~

The flight back to Toronto felt like it took no time at all. Austin and I sat next to each other and Brian even sweet-talked the gate agent into changing our seats so we were nowhere near the rest of the group. We had a lot to talk about: schedules to coordinate, training to plan, and we didn't need any distractions.

I would have to drop my classes and the internship for the rest of the year; we couldn't find any way around that. Hopefully, the university would let me defer to the following year given the extraordinary circumstances. Brian had already made some calls to Skate Canada while we were at the airport, and based on our junior record, they had no issue with allowing Austin and me to compete at the Canadian championships. We'd have to get new costumes made to fit me, and I already knew I'd want to make some changes to the dances to suit my own strengths and style rather than Grace's. The list of things to do went on and on, but the scheduling remained the most difficult part.

After nearly an hour of trying to arrange my life into a spreadsheet, Austin ran a hand through his hair in frustration. "The commute time is killing us. The university campus is too far from the rink, you're losing almost two hours a day in down time."

"I know, but I can't just get another apartment. I've already paid for the dorm for the year and I can't afford two places."

His frustrated expression morphed into a sly grin. "Well, there's a rather obvious alternative."

"Which is?" I asked warily. That grin could only mean trouble.

"Move in with me."

I studied him carefully, looking for any sign he might be joking, but although his eyes sparkled with excitement, nothing suggested he didn't mean it.

My heart swelled at the idea, but I tried to stay realistic. "That doesn't really support our 'no relationship' agreement."

"Why not? You can be my platonic housemate. I have two spare bedrooms, you can use one of them. You can also use my home gym and we can travel to the rink together. It makes sense, you know it does."

It did, I had to admit. The spreadsheet on my laptop made that perfectly clear. It would save time and money and it would be easier for me to stick to a strict training diet with a kitchen of my own rather than using the dorm's cafeteria. I could only see one down side: how could I live with Austin, knowing that I wanted him and knowing he wanted me, and not do anything about it?

It would be playing with fire, and I'd been burned once before. This time, I wouldn't let myself be distracted from the dream I'd been given an unexpected second chance at.

"We'll need some ground rules," I said, and Austin's face lit up at my implicit agreement. "No sex, obviously. That's rule number one."

He nodded. "I had a feeling you'd say that, which is why I suggested the separate bedrooms. What else?"

"No kissing either. No touching. No walking around the house naked. Nothing at all physically between us until after the Olympics."

That didn't go down as easily for him, but reluctantly, he gave his agreement. "I won't put any pressure on you, but if you change your mind at any time, I won't complain. Deal?"

He held out his hand and I shook it, trying to fight down the giddy excitement that threatened to overwhelm all my reason at the idea of sharing a home with the man of my dreams.

It looked like I had a new place to live.

By the time the plane landed, we had the next two months laid out, a road map to get us from that point all the way to the Canadian championships. The months ahead would be intense and demanding, but Austin had it right back at the hotel in Tokyo when he quoted my 13-year-old self back to me: as long as we put the work in, there was no reason we couldn't succeed.

~**Austin**~

The first week of living with Amy tested me even more than I expected it to. At night, I ran into her in the kitchen, wearing an adorable pair of pajamas that showed off her incredible body, and in the morning, I bumped into her coming out of the bathroom, wrapped in a towel after her post-workout shower. Even when she was fully dressed, every time I sat down next to her at the kitchen table or on the couch in the living room, I had to hold back from wrapping her up in my arms and picking up where we left off that night in the hot spring in Japan.

If I'd known that would be the last night I could kiss her for months, I definitely wouldn't have stopped when I did, hygiene rules in the water be damned.

Amy stopped wearing her glasses entirely since she couldn't wear them while working out or skating and she didn't really need them anyway. Between that and pulling her hair back to keep it out of her face, she looked more like the Amy I remembered, and she acted just like her too. She worked just as hard as I expected her to and returned home exhausted by the end of each day. I'd make us a healthy supper and we'd sit at the kitchen table talking through our plans for the next day. We never ran out of things to talk about, teasing and sparring with each other in a way that felt natural, familiar and exciting at the same time. In almost every way, it felt just like I always hoped it would when I imagined us being together.

Except for the fact that we weren't actually dating.

"Let's do the lift again," Brian instructed from the boards the following week. "Mia, you still need to lean forward a little more. Austin, your hand placement will help her get the leverage she needs. Move your hands a bit higher up her legs."

We turned away from him as I bit back a groan. "You know this is torture, right?" I said to her under my breath. "Getting closer to third base on the ice than we are off of it?"

Amy winked at me, not taking my complaint seriously. "You used to touch me like this all the time. And I was underage at the time."

I let the groan out that time. "You're not helping."

We ran the lift again, my hands higher between her legs, and Brian looked happier that time. "Better," he called out. "Keep practicing that off the ice."

"I would if I could," I muttered under my breath. Amy elbowed me in the ribs to shut me up, but her cheeks turned a little pink, letting me know that she had thought about it too.

Although we needed every day we had left for training, and a few more besides, in moments like those, I wished we could just skip straight to the Olympics and everything else that came afterwards.

~Amelia~

We arrived back at Austin's house after training a month before the Canadian championships, and I collapsed onto the couch with a sigh. "I thought I'd kept myself in pretty good shape in the last four years, but obviously not good enough. I must have been delusional."

My handsome housemate took a seat next to me, his eyes trailing up and down over my body. "Your shape looks pretty good to me."

My eye roll served as a defense mechanism, brushing off his comment because it was easier than acknowledging the tension that lay behind it. On the ice, I could laugh off the remarks he made, but at home, with just the two of us, resisting my attraction to him tested the limits of my self-control on a daily basis.

"Is that how you talk to all your skating partners?"

"Only the ones I want to sleep with."

A shiver of anticipation slithered its way down my spine as I bit my lip, trying not to react. "That's not exactly keeping things professional, Austin."

He let out a sigh, diffusing some of the electricity in the room as he slumped back into the sofa. "I know, but I didn't realize it would be quite this difficult. I want to be with you so badly. We're already living together and spending all of our time together. Would it really be so bad if we made out once in a while?"

I'd asked myself the same question a hundred times or more in the last month. Every night since I moved in, I tossed and turned in my bed, knowing Austin's room lay on the other side of the wall and that, at any time, I could go and knock on his door, and he wouldn't turn me away if I did.

And yet, each time, the voice of 13-year-old Amy in the back of my head held me back. *No distractions. Focus on the medal.* What if we gave into our desires and were disappointed? What if we weren't honest with each other on the ice because we didn't want to hurt each other's feelings? With so many potential pitfalls, a few weeks before the biggest competition of our lives didn't seem like the best time to take that risk. The first time we kissed, my whole life fell apart the next day. That exact scenario might not happen again, but there were too many other variables to account for.

We'd waited so long already. A little bit longer wouldn't kill us, though sometimes, late at night, it felt like it might.

Thankfully, he didn't expect me to answer his question. Instead, he held out his hands. "Give me your feet."

The sudden change threw me off and I blinked up at him in confusion. "What?"

"You've been wearing your skates way more than you're used to," he reminded me, as if I didn't know that from how they'd been aching. "Let me rub them for you."

That sounded like heaven. Even if my brain thought I should say no, my body had already begun to twist on the couch before I could talk myself out of it. He grabbed my ankles as I raised my legs and laid them gently across his lap before digging his knuckle into the arch of one.

A loud moan shot through my lips and Austin paused, shifting in his seat and moving my other foot further down his legs. "I'm trying so hard to be good here, Amy. You've got to cut me some slack."

"Sorry." I tried not to grin as he resumed his massage, biting my lip to suppress the other sounds that wanted to come out.

"Brian asked me today what we're doing about media," he said as his fingers worked their magic on my feet. "Without my mom, we don't have anyone managing that."

We'd been so focused on skating since returning from Japan, everything else had fallen to the wayside. Ben's article about me had been overshadowed by the much bigger news of Grace's suspension. People were probably curious about Austin and I skating together, but giving in to requests for interviews would only take time away from our training. We needed every spare minute we had.

"They've been trying to reach Brian since they can't get us," Austin explained further. "He's happy to ignore it, but he wanted to let us know."

"I think we should ignore it too," I suggested, my breath catching as Austin hit a particularly tight spot in my foot. "We don't even know for certain that we'll be ready for Canadians."

His snort sounded almost like mine when I laughed. "You'll have us both whipped into shape in plenty of time and you know it. Be honest with me: what's the real reason you don't want to talk to the press?"

With a sigh, I let my head fall back onto the couch cushion. "I guess I just don't want to tempt fate. What if they do a big story on us and we don't end up competing? A lot could happen between now and then. I'd rather fly under the radar for as long as possible."

Although I didn't say it, the parallels between my reasons for avoiding the media and for not jumping into a relationship with Austin were pretty much the same. Both were unpredictable. What happened on the ice and with my body, I had some control over, through sheer force of will. Everything else was out of my hands, and that kind of terrified me.

I knew I would never get another shot at this. I hadn't even expected to have this one, and I didn't want to mess it up in any way.

"If that's what you want, I support you completely," he promised. "No media."

"In or out," I added. "I don't want to know what's happening with other skaters either. Let's stick to focusing on the things we can change. We'll have our own little cocoon, insulated from the rest of the world."

"I like the sounds of that."

His strong fingers rubbed my heel as he shot me a teasing smile.

"I'd like it more if there was some kissing going on in that cocoon."

His persistence made me laugh, and he let out an exaggerated sigh that I knew he didn't really mean.

"Alright. Stay here and relax, I'll get us something to eat."

He put my feet gently down on the couch and left for the kitchen. His skills as a cook came as a surprise to me and we were having fun cooking together most nights. In fact, we had fun doing just about everything together. Living with him exceeded even my most optimistic expectations, other than those long, frustrating nights apart from him.

Only a few more months to go, I reminded myself. A few more long, long months.

~**Austin**~

Four days before Christmas, Amy had just finished setting the table when the doorbell rang. She practically squealed in anticipation. "I'll get it. Are you ready?"

"Do I have a choice?" I asked drily and she shot me a teasing glare.

"Not anymore. Don't worry, they'll be on their best behaviour."

She skipped down the small staircase of the split-level house to open the door to her university friends while I smiled at her retreating back, loving the chance to see her so excited.

We weren't going to be seeing our parents for Christmas, too busy with training and still not over the betrayal we'd suffered from them, so Amy had decided to invite her friends over for a holiday meal. Although I'd heard all about them over the past six weeks, that night would be the first time I met them in person. I had a feeling the 'Mia' they knew was quite different from the Amy I saw on the ice, and I couldn't wait to see another side of the woman I got to know a little better every day.

After giving them a couple of minutes to say hello and get their winter coats and boots off, I made my way to the top of the stairs. "Can I get anyone a drink?"

Three pairs of curious eyes locked on me while Amy did her best to hide her smile.

"White wine," the one who had to be Gaby said. Based on Amy's stories, I felt like I knew her already.

"Make that two. And I'm Jenna, by the way."

By process of elimination, that left Rosa. "As long as you keep making Mia beam like this, you can make me anything you like."

Her declaration sent all four women into giggles.

"White wine for everyone, then," I announced, leaving them to their whispers and laughter.

Over our meal, Amy refused to let me answer any of the other women's questions until they'd filled her in on their lives, but after that, they had free rein to ask me anything and everything, and nobody held back.

"How weird is it to have people you've never met in love with you?" Rosa asked first.

"She's been deep diving into the skating boards online," Jenna added in explanation, her second glass of wine in her hand as she gestured. "Some of those people are pretty enthusiastic."

"I don't really spend much time thinking about it, to be honest. I appreciate the support of our fans, but none of them are truly in love with me. They don't actually know me."

"That sounds like a rehearsed answer," Amy teased. "Come on, guys, give him a tough one."

"I've got one," Jenna announced. "If you could know the results of a competition ahead of time, would you want to?"

That *was* a more interesting question. "You mean if someone could tell me right now how we would do at Canadians?"

"Exactly. Would you want to know or not?"

My eyes drifted to Amy as I thought it over. She'd had a glass of wine too, unusually for her while we were training, and the alcohol had tinted her cheeks a pretty shade of pink. Her blue eyes watched me curiously, waiting for my answer along with the others.

"I wouldn't want to know. If I found out we did well, it might diminish the competitive edge that pushes me. If I found out we didn't do well, I might lose motivation. It's better not knowing."

In Amy's nod of agreement, I could see we were perfectly aligned in that perspective, as in most things.

"My turn," Gaby interjected. "How in the world did you not recognize Amy when she came to interview you?"

The others all broke into laughter while I groaned. "She looked really different," I protested, knowing full well that wouldn't satisfy them.

It didn't. In response, Rosa took off her cardigan and wrapped it over Amy's head like a shawl. "Do you recognize her now?"

"No, she needs the glasses, like Clark Kent!" Jenna giggled, and when Amy laughed so hard that she snorted, the whole room rang with the women's laughter and good-natured jibes.

Eventually, the teasing stopped, and I tried to add a fuller explanation. "All joking aside, it seemed so incredibly unlikely that she would be there that even when things about Mia seemed familiar to me, I found other explanations for them. After being disappointed so many times over so many years, I convinced myself that I would never see Amy again, and I think it created a mental block I couldn't see past, no matter how much I should have been able to. I couldn't believe I'd be lucky enough to have her back in my life again."

That earned me a chorus of 'awww's that *almost* made up for the earlier mockery.

Jenna asked one more question before we moved on. "What about Grace? Are you guys still friends?"

My eyes met Amy's again, the curiosity in her expression even stronger than before. We'd been so focused on everything we needed to do to achieve our goal that Grace had barely crossed my mind. Knowing how abandoned Amy felt when she couldn't skate anymore, perhaps I should have been making more of an effort.

"We haven't been talking very much, but I would like for us to be friends."

With that in mind, when the women all left for the night, I sent Grace a text.

> Hey. I hope you're doing okay. If you need to talk about anything, I'm here. Have a good Christmas.

By the time I went to bed, I could see that she read the message but didn't respond so I put it out of my mind for the time being. The ball was in her court; if she wanted to reach out, she could, and in the meantime, my focus would remain on Amy and the challenges we still had ahead of us in the coming months.

Chapter Ten

~**Amelia**~

The two weeks after Christmas flew by even faster than the ones before had, and almost before I knew it, the time arrived for us to travel to Ottawa for the Canadian championships. The fact that the competition that year would be taking place in the city where Austin and I trained together for so many years felt like a sign from the universe, hopefully a good one, and we decided to drive up together from Toronto rather than flying. It let us avoid the airport crowds and any potential media attention, keeping our focus purely on the competition where it should be.

My dad and his new family bought tickets to see us perform and my mom would be making the trip from St John's too. Things still weren't fully back to normal between us but she didn't want to miss out on such a big moment in my life, so I agreed that she could come even though I couldn't promise that we would have any time to spend with her.

"Will your mom be there?" I asked Austin from the passenger seat of his car, the Trans-Canada Highway stretching out in front of us.

"She bought herself tickets, but she won't be backstage," he promised. "Don't worry about her."

He still hadn't told me exactly what they argued about in Japan, only that things had already deteriorated between them even before the mess with Grace. What she thought about us competing together again, I could only guess at, but in the end, it didn't matter. Everything off the ice was a distraction, and we'd worked too hard for the last two months to let anything come between us and the performance I knew we could give.

"We're going to win this, you know," Austin added, his hand reaching over to find mine on my lap. "We're going to blow everyone away."

"I hope so."

His hand squeezed mine, its weight so familiar and comfortable but also new and exciting. "Hope? That's not the Amy I know. Where's that girl who's going to win the Olympic gold medal?"

"She's a little bit terrified about competing for the first time in five years," I admitted. "The crowds, the judges, the cameras, the attention, all of it. It's been a long time."

"I know." His warm, comforting voice matched the affectionate look in his eyes as he glanced over at me. "But you're ready for this, and I'm right beside you. You're not doing it on your own. We're a team. And more than that, we're the team that's going to win this thing."

His certainty brought a smile to my face, the first real smile of the day. Somehow, our usual roles had reversed, but I didn't mind. Just this one, I could lean on his confidence and experience, and the way he made the whole outcome sound like a foregone conclusion.

Just two dances and we'd be Canadian champions.

What did I have to worry about?

~Austin~

Sticking to our plan of eliminating all external distractions, Brian arranged for private practice time for us in Ottawa except for the final practice session. That last session, at the official competition venue, would be our one chance to get a feel for the ice and make any last-minute adjustments we needed to for our performance. Ice could be softer or harder depending on the temperature of the arena, the thickness of the ice, and other little factors that affected the ease at which our blades cut across the surface. It would be the final piece of the puzzle we needed to put together our ultimate performance.

Amy's knee bounced nervously as we pulled into the parking lot for the final practice session. I'd never seen her so worked up about a competition before, but in a strange way, the more uncertain she seemed, the more confident I felt. The next-best team placed eighth at the previous year's World championships where Grace and I finished second, and Amy was a better dancer than Grace. That might have sounded like bias to her so I didn't say it out loud, but having skated with both of them, I considered it an irrefutable fact.

We were the best dancers at the competition and we were going to win.

Along with testing the ice, we also decided to run the practice in costume to make it feel as real as possible, and when Amy came out of the changing room, her lips were drawn even tighter than before.

"Tell me the truth: how bad does it look?"

It took me a moment to figure out what she meant. At first glance, I thought she looked incredible in the green dress that had been retailored to fit her rather than Grace, but eventually, I realized she meant the scar on her leg, visible beneath the sheer nylons she wore.

"It's noticeable," I answered honestly since she'd asked for the truth. "But it doesn't look bad."

I hated the idea of the pain it had caused her and everything she'd been through, especially since I hadn't been there to support her through it, but I also found it a symbol of her incredible strength and perseverance. Ultimately, it was another part of her, beautiful in its own way.

"Trust me: once you start moving, nobody's going to pay any attention to it."

She offered me a small smile of appreciation as she slipped her hand in mine and we headed together down the hall from the change room to the ice.

"It sounds loud out there," Amy whispered as we approached the opening that led to the side of the rink where the other skaters in our session already waited to take the ice.

"It does," I had to agree. The public could buy tickets to see the official practice sessions but usually, attendance didn't come close to the actual competition. That day, however, we were greeted with almost a full house when we stepped out onto the ice.

We'd expected a bit of extra interest given the news about Grace's suspension and Amy's return, but as Amy wanted, we'd purposefully avoided all media and fan forums while we were training. She wouldn't even let Jenna tell her about things she read online. As a result, the sheer number of cameras pointed in our direction took us both by surprise and tension radiated through Amy's body as we stroked around the ice to warm up.

"Ignore them," I murmured, giving her hand a squeeze. "This is about us. No one else."

She nodded, taking a deep breath as she did her best to relax.

A few moments later, the announcer began reading out the names of the skaters on the ice, and when he got to us - Mia Wilson and Austin Black - we got a reaction I'd never had in all my years of competing.

The crowd *booed*.

Not all of them, certainly, but enough that we were clearly able to hear it over the cheers.

My stomach seemed to fill with lead as my eyes met Amy's, shock reflecting back at me in her pretty blue irises.

"Ignore it," I said, trying to sound more confident than I felt. "We've got a job to do here, let's focus on that."

Brian repeated those sentiments when we headed over to him at the boards after completing the warm up. "Nobody in those stands is determining whether or not you two win this thing. It's entirely up to you."

Amy and I both nodded at each other, our determination pushing past the uncertainty, and for the rest of the practice, we tuned out everything else around us. If the crowd booed again, we didn't hear it. If they cheered, we missed that too. All I heard was the sound of my breathing and hers and the swish of our blades slicing through the ice. All I felt was her body beneath my hands, sure and strong, every step where it should be.

The ice turned out to be perfect for us, very close to the conditions we trained on in our regular club, and by the time the session ended, I felt good about our prospects for the next day. The crowd applauded as all the skaters left the ice, the earlier jeers all but forgotten.

Backstage, a few reporters were waiting, and we were expected to speak with them. The first two, we gave stock answers to all the questions, talking about how happy we were to be skating together again and whether or not we'd worked out all our nerves during the practice session that day. Neither of them asked about Grace, which I appreciated.

The third reporter, however, was none other than Ben Miller.

Amy had filled me in on everything that happened in Japan, and I knew I had nothing to worry about from her side, but the thought of him hitting on her, *kissing* her, still made me a little crazy. However, I knew we would see him at this event; he had a job to do just like we did, so I'd prepared for this moment as much as I could. Amy and I both greeted him politely while his cameraman got set up, and once they were rolling, Ben turned to us with a warm smile.

"Everyone has been waiting to get a glimpse of the newly re-formed team of Wilson and Black, and I have to say: you looked great out there today. Mia, how did it feel for you to be back in front of a crowd after so many years?"

She flashed me a quick smile before answering him. "It felt really good. With Austin, it's easy to forget about everything else and be comfortable with the program. We're confident the rest of the week will go well too."

I knew she didn't feel quite as confident as she sounded, but I admired the conviction she conveyed.

"Comfortable is a great word," Ben agreed smoothly. "It looked like you guys have been doing this for years, not months. Austin, what's it like to be back on the ice with Mia?"

"It's like nothing's changed. She's still just as amazing as always, and I'm so lucky that she stepped in to skate with me for the rest of this season."

That seemed to give him the opening he'd been waiting for. "Well, we do need to talk about that, don't we? This whole situation is incredibly unusual, especially in figure skating. How are you two managing to stay focused with all the rumours and speculation going around?"

Amy and I exchanged uncertain glances. If he was referring to specific rumours, we didn't know what they were, so I answered for both of us. "We don't pay attention to rumours. We've been too busy training. That's taken up all of our time."

"Of course," Ben agreed, but I could see before he even opened his mouth again that he wouldn't leave it there. "But Mia, I have to ask: is there any truth to the things Grace Matthews has been saying?"

Once again, Amy looked up at me for direction, and I could only shrug. "I'm afraid I don't know what she's been saying," she answered, turning back to Ben with her smile still on, though now strained more than before. "We really haven't been following it."

To his credit, Ben looked genuinely surprised. He must have expected her to have some answer prepared and when she didn't, he almost looked like he didn't want to continue. However, he stuck to his script, just as we stuck to ours. "Well, I think everyone who knows you already knows the answer, but maybe you could just confirm for the people at home: were you the one responsible for Grace taking that medication in Tokyo?"

~Amelia~

Time seemed to stop as soon as Ben asked the question and I could only blink at him, stupefied.

People blamed me for Grace taking the banned medication? Did Grace say I had something to do with it? What exactly *did* she say?

Maybe I should have been paying attention to the media and online gossip after all.

A million things raced through my mind but none of them were a coherent answer to Ben's question. In fact, I couldn't seem to put *any* words together. My mouth opened and closed uselessly a couple of times until, to my great relief, Austin stepped in and answered for me.

"That's a completely ridiculous idea." Anger bled through his tone despite his obvious attempt to control it. "Grace made her own decisions. I'm just grateful and so lucky that Amy could step in and skate with me again so I didn't lose the whole season. Thank you."

The dismissal couldn't be clearer, and Ben signalled to the cameraman to cut while Austin put his arm around me and pulled me away, leading me towards the locker room.

"Wait, hang on," Ben called out from behind us. We turned back to see him jogging up to us, a frown on his face. "I'm sorry about that, I didn't mean to ambush you. Didn't your PR person prep you for that question?"

Once again, Austin and I exchanged glances, communicating more with our eyes than most people could with an entire conversation. Since he fired his mom, we didn't have anyone handling publicity for us. It hadn't seemed important compared to all the work we needed to do on the ice, but we hadn't anticipated anything like this.

"You really don't know what everyone's been talking about?" Ben continued, his eyebrows raised incredulously.

"Did Grace actually say I gave her the medication?" I asked, my voice sounding strained and tight.

Was that why people booed us before? Did they all think I'd sabotaged her on purpose? Were they all convinced, like Mrs Black seemed to be, that I'd only ever been out for myself?

"No, not exactly." Ben ran a hand through his hair, leaving it artfully ruffled. "My producer and I agreed to phrase it that way to make it clear how silly the whole thing sounds."

"What did Grace say, exactly?" Austin demanded, his anger still simmering.

Ben grimaced, his shoulders lifting in an apologetic shrug. "She gave an interview where they quoted her saying that Mia was the reason that she took the medication. Personally, I suspect her words were taken out of context, but she never clarified what she meant and some people have decided that it means Mia gave her the pills or told her to take them. There are quite a few conspiracy theories floating around. People have some crazy imaginations."

That didn't make me feel much better and Ben seemed to recognize that as he looked back over at me.

"Look, I don't want to tell you what to do, but it might help for the public to hear your side of this too, to clear things up once and for all."

"So you can have another exclusive story?" Austin's arm tightened around me protectively. "What happens off the ice is our business. Our lives aren't for anyone's entertainment or to help your career."

"Austin."

I said his name quietly, putting my hand on his arm to let him know how much I appreciated his support. However, I also didn't think Ben had any ulterior motives, as Austin seemed to.

I gave Ben a tight smile. "We'll think about it. For now, we need to focus on tomorrow."

"Of course," he agreed. "You know where to find me if you do want to talk. And you guys really did look great out there. Good luck tomorrow."

He walked away while Austin and I turned back to each other, the uncertainty I felt reflected back at me in his expression, even as he tried to give me a smile. "It doesn't affect what's happening on the ice. The judges are only judging what they see."

Even though the words sounded good, I could hear the lack of conviction in his voice. If the crowd thought I had done something dirty and underhanded, maybe some of the judges thought so too, which might affect the way they marked us. After all, if Austin truly didn't care what the judges thought, why would he have bothered to pretend to date Grace for so long in the first place?

Suddenly, it felt like everyone was rooting for us to fail.

From the moment I woke up the next day, nothing seemed to go right.

To kick things off, I managed to trip getting out of bed in the morning.

"Damn it!" I swore as my arm crashed against the bedside table. Knowing my body as well as I did, I knew a bruise would swell up in no time, and I'd have to try my best to cover it with makeup before our performance that afternoon.

Austin and I worked out together in the hotel gym in the morning, and somehow, my foot slipped getting off the treadmill. I hit the ground hard, leaving my backside a little bruised too, though at least no one would see that one. "You were never superstitious before," Austin reminded me when we met up for lunch in the hotel restaurant after we both showered and changed. "You always said we make our own luck."

His eyes drifted to the four-leaf clover necklace sitting just below my collarbone.

"That's what I'm afraid of," I told him bluntly. "Am I doing this? Am I sabotaging myself?"

I'd never been clumsy, so two falls in one day before we even stepped on the ice seemed like some kind of warning.

"Here we go," the waitress interrupted, setting our plates down in front of us. "Can I get you anything else?"

The grilled sandwiches she placed in front of us smelled great, but were definitely *not* what we ordered. "We both had grilled chicken salads," Austin pointed out, his brows knitted together in confusion. "Not sandwiches."

"Are you sure?"

The conversation seemed to attract attention, and as people realized who we were, whispers began to spread around the room. Everywhere I looked, people seemed to be staring at us. By the time he convinced her we had definitely ordered salads, the sandwiches were taken away and the salads brought out, I'd lost my appetite.

"Do you want to hang out until it's time to go to the rink?" Austin asked once his empty plate and my picked-over meal had been taken away.

"I think I'd rather be alone," I told him honestly. "I'm just going to have a rest, safe in my bed where nothing else can go wrong."

Back in my room, I tried to nap, but my mind refused to switch off. Finally, against all my better judgement, I pulled out my computer to look up exactly what people had been saying about me, and quickly wished I hadn't.

Things were even worse than I could have imagined.

On the plus side, some people did try to defend me, but a very vocal group of Grace's fans seemed convinced that I had orchestrated everything from the beginning: sweet-talking my way back into Austin's life, pretending to be Grace's friend so she would agree to me working with them, and arranging for her to take the medication in Tokyo that led to her suspension.

In some versions of events, I replaced her actual cold medication with a version that had been spiked. In others, I simply offered it to her, pretending to be helping while plotting her downfall.

Karma will get her, one person wrote. *Can't wait to see them crash and burn at Canadians.*

By the time Austin knocked on my door so we could head to the arena, I was wound up tighter than I could ever remember being.

"It's going to be okay," he said, his hands attempting to massage away some of the tension in my shoulders as we rode in the taxi to the arena. "We can't control what people are saying, but we *can* control how we do out there today. Let's blow them all away, and the rest won't matter."

Although I nodded, the lump in my throat refused to go away.

After changing into my costume backstage, I began lacing my skates, the same way I'd done a million times before. Maybe I pulled too hard, or perhaps the lace had already begun to fray, and somehow, it snapped apart in my hands.

Luckily, Brian always carried an extra pair, and I was able to get them relaced before our warm-up, but once we were announced, I heard the random boos scattered through the crowd and tears pricked my eyes. It had been one thing after another all day long.

For years, I had dreamt of this moment, and never once did I imagine it going this way.

We were the first team to skate after the warm-up, and as we circled each other in the centre of the ice, Austin took my face in his hands. "It's just you and me here right now. I believe in you, Amy."

Unfortunately, that wasn't entirely true. Aside from the two of us, cameras captured our every move to beam into living rooms across the country, not to mention the thousands of people in the arena and the row of judges right in front of us.

My legs trembled as we took our starting positions, my smile strained and false.

The music swelled around us, Austin pulled me into his arms to begin, and somehow, I completely lost my balance.

I couldn't even say how it happened. My feet simply went out from under me, and as he tried to catch me, Austin stumbled too.

We both ended up on the ice, mere seconds into the program.

The sound of ten thousand people gasping in unison filled the air as we both scrambled back to our feet, my cheeks flushed red and my heart pounding in shock and disbelief.

By the time we caught up to the music, the crowd had started to applaud, trying to encourage us, but I couldn't help thinking of the people on those message boards I'd read earlier that day, the people who would be happy to see us struggling and feel that we deserved it.

I did my best to shut my brain off for the rest of the program, going through the motions on auto-pilot. We ticked off the remaining elements, one by one, with no glaring technical errors, but it felt cold and robotic even to me. It must have come across that way too, given the crowd's muted reaction.

We were capable of so much more.

Austin pulled me into a tight hug as soon as the music ended. "It's okay, Amy. Seriously. It's a good enough program that we'll be fine. Don't worry about it."

He'd been through enough ups and downs during his career to be able to bounce back from a bad performance, but I knew he must be disappointed too, no matter how much he tried to cover it up.

In the kiss 'n' cry area, we did our best to keep smiling, and our marks actually weren't as bad as they could have been. We were in third place, still within striking distance of the other two teams, and a good performance in the free dance could still mean a win. As long as we finished in the top three, we had a chance of being named to the Olympic team, so it wasn't a complete disaster by any means.

It only felt that way.

Somehow, we made it through the post-performance interviews, doing our best to laugh off the shaky opening. By the time we completed all our post-competition obligations and made it back to the hotel, I was ready to crawl back into my bed and pretend the whole day had never happened.

"I'm just going to get some room service tonight," I told Austin as I opened my hotel room door. "I don't feel like going out to eat."

He didn't argue, but when I walked inside the room, he followed after me.

"What are you...?"

Before I could finish the question, his mouth was on mine.

This kiss had nothing in common with either of the two kisses we shared in the past. Those had been tentative and exploring, but this felt hard and demanding, his lips bruising mine with their fierceness as his hands gripped my head. With my gasp of surprise, I inhaled the familiar scent of his cologne, its aroma as appealing as always but now laced with a strong hit of desire. I melted into him, clinging to him almost desperately as I felt both the passion and the support driving the movement of his mouth on mine.

When he finally pulled back, both of us breathing deeply, his eyes pierced into mine with a determination I'd never seen before, not even on the ice.

"We said we wouldn't do this because it could mess things up, right?"

I didn't need to ask what he meant by 'this'. I couldn't think of anything besides the way he just kissed me and the electricity still pulsing between us.

Unable to form any words, I simply nodded my understanding.

"Well, they're already messed up. If tonight's performance is what we get from waiting, then I'm done waiting. If this is how we're going down, we might as well enjoy the ride."

A shiver raced down my spine, every nerve in my body alive with anticipation. Every reason I had for believing that we needed to wait, every fear about what might or might not happen on the ice drained away until all I could see or hear or feel or want was *him*.

"You're my other half, Amy. You always have been, on and off the ice. The whole time you were away from me, half of me was missing, and being so close to you but not being able to make you mine entirely is killing me. For once, let's just say: 'screw the rest of the world'. Screw the skating and the judges and everything else. No more waiting, no more hiding, no more missed chances. All I want is right here in this room. All I want is..."

I'd heard enough.

Before he could finish, my hand wrapped around the back of his neck and pulled his mouth back down to mine. No words were necessary: he was right, and I didn't want to wait anymore either.

All the unrequited love of my teenage years, all the time spent missing him during the four years we were apart and all the frustration of being so close to him the last few months but unable to do anything about it, all of it boiled up and over into the most passionate and intense night of my life.

I had been with other men before and I knew Austin had been with other women, but I also knew without him telling me that this night was different, just as special to him as to me.

As his arms wrapped around me afterwards, our bodies as perfectly in sync as they always had been on the ice, Austin whispered in my ear, "This is better than any gold medal."

"Tell me that again after we win one."

He grinned before kissing me again, our night not over yet.

More than seven years after we first met, Austin was finally mine, and I knew one thing with utter certainty, knew it more clearly than I had ever known anything before.

This was only the beginning.

Chapter Eleven

~Austin~

For a moment when I woke up the next morning, I was afraid to open my eyes.

It wouldn't have been the first time I dreamed about being with Amy only to wake up and realize it had only been in my head. If the night before had been a dream, I didn't want to know. I'd rather linger in the warmth of that memory as long as possible before reality crashed back in.

However, when I finally gathered the courage to blink my eyes open, they focused on the woman asleep on the pillow next to me, and my heart swelled with happiness.

It really happened. Amy and I spent the night together and the world didn't end. If anything, it felt more full of possibilities than ever before. She looked beautiful in the soft morning light, her face relaxed in sleep. Her eyelashes sat gently against her skin, her cheeks tinted a pale pink from the heat of the warm bed covers, and her lips were slightly parted. Although I didn't want to wake her, I couldn't keep from touching her either. Leaning over, I placed a gentle, light kiss on her lips, and her eyelids fluttered open.

The smile that spread across her face when she saw me had to be the most breathtaking thing I had ever seen. "What time is it?" she whispered, glancing over her shoulder towards the window and the morning sun filtering in through the curtains.

"Nearly ten." The TV had a digital clock built in so I could answer without checking my phone. "Guess we wore each other out last night."

Her cheeks flushed a deeper shade of pink but her eyes filled with a happiness at the memories of the night before that mirrored my own. It had been incredible, just as amazing as I ever could have imagined, and at long last, we were truly partners in every sense of the word.

I didn't regret it for a second, and it relieved me to see that she didn't either.

Amy pulled herself up, propping her back up against the headboard. "Maybe we should give Ben a call before the free dance."

My eyebrows shot up. "You're thinking about him while you're in bed with me? You really are going to give me some kind of a complex, Amy."

"Not like that, you idiot."

With a laugh, I kissed her again, loving that she felt comfortable enough to tell me off in private just like she would have on the ice. Finally, I had the best of her in both worlds.

"Like what, then?"

"To see if we can do an interview. Tell our side of the story, like he suggested."

As much as I didn't want to spend any time with anyone else until we absolutely had to, I had to admit that it might be a good idea to do something proactive about the whole situation. People were only buying into the conspiracy theories about Grace because they hadn't been given any other information to go on. If we told our truth, some people might not believe it, but at least they'd have that choice.

I groaned my agreement and Amy pulled out her phone to make the call.

"My network will be thrilled to get an exclusive interview," he assured us. "It'll be included in tonight's broadcast. Can you meet me at the arena in an hour?"

Amy agreed, turning to me as soon as she hung up. "I'm going to have a quick shower. You should go get ready too."

"You're sure you don't want me to join you?" I didn't want to be away from her a second longer than I needed to be.

She scrunched up her nose at me. "Not if we need to be there in an hour! But after the free dance tonight, I'm all yours."

With another groan of both desire and frustration, I let her go and went back to my own room to get ready.

An hour later, an assistant clipped mics onto our shirts, two cameras trained on us as Ben sat down across from us. "Are you guys ready for this?" he asked.

Amy and I exchanged glances, giving each other a supportive smile. "Ready as we'll ever be," she replied, taking my hand.

For the next hour, Ben asked us questions about our past, about our partnership, and about what happened in Tokyo. We answered them all as honestly as we could. I tried not to sound too much like I blamed Grace for what had happened, even though it had been entirely her decision. I focused instead on just how lucky I was to have Amy available and willing to skate with me again, and how I couldn't wait to skate with her at the Olympics, just like we had planned to do all those years ago.

"And what about afterwards?" Ben asked. "Grace's suspension will be lifted next year, so which partner will you choose to skate with then?"

I kept my expression as neutral as possible beneath the studio lights. "The one thing the past few years have taught me is that you can't control the future. Things come out of the blue, things that you never saw coming. All I'm worried about is right here and now, going out today and skating the best free dance we can, and hopefully representing our country at the Olympics and putting in the performance we always wanted to out there."

Ben nodded. "And Amy? I mean, Mia, sorry. What are your long-term plans?"

Her confident smile filled me with pride. The nerves of the past few days seemed to have vanished as she took control of her own narrative again. "Like Austin, I'm not thinking much past today, just taking each day as it comes. Any day that I get to wake up and get on the ice is good enough for me."

After a few more questions, he wrapped it up, the cameras turned off and Ben shot us an encouraging smile. "That was brilliant. The team here will edit it right away, and we'll run clips from it just before you skate tonight. It won't be in time to sway the crowd in the arena but the folks at home will love it."

"Thanks, Ben. We appreciate your help."

I offered my hand to him and he shook it with a hint of the smirk that had always gotten under my skin.

"It's not purely out of the goodness of my heart. This is my first exclusive interview on camera, and as you pointed out the other day, it'll look good for me too. But I honestly *am* rooting for you guys. Hope you go out there today and show them what you've really got."

"We will," Amy and I said in unison, completely back on the same page.

After the interview, we still had some time to kill and as much as I would have loved to spend it back at the hotel, it would be better to wait until after the competition so we didn't have to worry about being anywhere or losing track of time. At her suggestion, Amy and I drove over to our old club, the rink where we skated together for those three years when we were younger.

After spending a bit of time inside, we returned to the parking lot, but instead of heading to the car, Amy took my hand, leading us a couple of blocks away before stopping halfway down the street.

"This is where it happened."

She pointed at the pavement just ahead of us while my mind scrambled to catch up, trying to figure out what she meant.

"That's what it said on the police report, at least. The car jumped the curb just here." She pointed down at the nondescript edge of the sidewalk, nothing about it looking any different from any other curb in any other city. "It knocked me off the sidewalk and into the yard of this house."

She gestured at the brick house to our left while a thick lump filled my throat. Even after all this time, I still knew so little about the details of her accident, and the idea of her lying on the ground, her body broken, all alone, hit me harder than I expected it to. It hurt me to even think about it, but I wanted all the details.

"Who called the ambulance?" My voice shook with the question but she didn't react to it, keeping her gaze forward.

"There were a couple of other pedestrians, just down the street." She gestured ahead of us again, as if the people were still there. "They came running over, I guess. I was unconscious so I don't remember any of this. The driver was an older man in his eighties, and he hit a patch of black ice on the street and lost control. Apparently, he was distraught. He came to visit me in the hospital, you know."

Another pang of grief shot through me. I hadn't known that, actually. How would I? It stung like a fresh cut on an old scar to find out her mom let the driver who hit her see her, but not me.

When would that ever stop hurting?

Amy kept talking, still looking at the ground rather than at me. "For a long time, I thought my dreams ended right here on this street, but not anymore. You've given them all back to me, Austin. Even if we don't win today, just being here with you, skating again, competing again, and especially being with you last night... it's been everything I could have ever wished for."

My arms went around her, pulling her tight against me. "If we come out of this weekend with just you and me being together, that would be good enough for me, but that's not what's going to happen. We're going to go out there today and we're going to win this thing, and we're going to go get that gold medal next month too. You know how I know?"

At last, she looked up at me, letting me see the tears in her eyes. There was some sadness in her expression, a lingering sadness I understood completely, but beyond it, I could see acceptance. Peace. Hope.

"How do you know?"

"Because seven years ago, on that ice just a few blocks away from here, you told me so." I wiped the tears with my thumbs and tilted her face upwards, bending down to kiss her lips. In that kiss was every promise I had ever made her, along with one new one.

No matter how I let her down in the past, I wouldn't fail her again.

We were finally going to get our happy ending.

~Amelia~

When Austin and I walked back into the arena that evening, we were a completely different team than we had been the night before. No one else existed, as far as we were concerned. As we went through our off-ice warm-up, I didn't see or hear anyone around us. We kept our focus on each other, and on the promise we'd made to each other standing on the street that afternoon, at the spot where everything fell apart so many years ago.

No matter what happened that night, we were going to skate the program for each other. This was our dream and no one got to decide how it would go except for us.

When we finally got on the ice for our warm-up, Austin circled the outside of the ice like he always did while I did my sculling, feeling the ice, testing my legs. Once again, I blocked out everything else around me. If there were boos or cheers from the crowd, I didn't hear them. But when Austin came to join me to begin our joint warm-up, he surprised me by pointing up into the crowd.

"Look at that sign up there."

I followed the direction of his point to the end of the rink where a large banner hung from the second tier of seats. It read: *We love you Austin and Amy / Mia!*

The inclusion of both my names struck me as so silly that I couldn't help laughing. "It sounds like I have some kind of multiple personality disorder."

Austin chuckled too. "We've still got people behind us," he reminded me as we began our stroking routine. "But we're not worrying about them or the haters either. Tonight, it's just you and me."

At the idea of just me and him, the memories of our bodies tangled together last night flashed across my mind, and I had to bite back a grin, looking down at the ice so no one could see me blush.

Austin and I were the last team to skate in our group, the last team to skate for the whole event, so when our warm-up ended, we put our skate guards back on and headed back to the locker room. When we competed together when we were younger, we never really spoke much during this time, but that night, Austin cracked jokes and reminded me of things that happened during our training years ago that had completely slipped my mind.

By the time the volunteer came to tell us we could get ready to go back out, I had almost forgotten what we were there for, but one look at Austin's face and all the promises, past and present, came flooding back.

The arena went silent as we took our starting positions on the ice. I exhaled one long, last breath as Austin gave me a wink. "Let's show them how it's done."

From the first step, I knew this skate would be nothing like the one the night before.

The rhythm of the music flowed through me, from the tips of my fingers straight through my body and down to my toes, and I couldn't have put a foot wrong even if I wanted to. In that instant, Mia and Amy ceased to exist. I became the character in the story I wanted to tell in the program I created, and Austin, looking more handsome than ever in his soldier's uniform, became the man I loved but was destined to lose.

Every experience of the last four years, each moment of hope and each heartbreak, poured into my movements. As Austin lifted me up, rather than seeing the crowd in Ottawa in front of me, I could see the distance that separated us instead. Every time our eyes connected, I felt both the joy of finding my soulmate and the pain of losing him, and I could see it reflected in his face too.

The crowd must have made some noise as we skated, but I didn't hear anything. All I knew in that moment was the dance, the perfect way that Austin's every move complemented mine, the way each element felt new even though we'd done them a dozen times every day for the last two months.

And when it finally ended, Austin with his arms outstretched and me slumped across them, representing the death of the characters, a great weight lifted from my shoulders.

That was the program we wanted to skate.

Whether we won or not, we couldn't have done anything more. I skated it for him and he did it for me, just like we said.

Austin lifted my head gently, wrapping his arms around me as we hugged each other tightly. "That was perfect," I told him, though I knew I didn't need to say it. He would have felt it too.

"You're perfect," was his reply, whispered in my ear.

Only after we separated did I realize that the crowd was on their feet, giving us a full standing ovation. The noise of the cheers finally pierced through the walls I'd built around myself, and the sound washed over me, nearly knocking me over and filling me with pride and happiness as Austin and I took our bows.

The crowd continued to cheer as we made our way to the kiss 'n' cry area, hugging Brian along the way. Austin pulled him over to sit down with us.

"It's first," Brian assured us, his smile relieved and proud and gratified all at the same time. "You won, I promise."

As much as I wanted to believe it, I couldn't until the marks came up. When they finally did, my jaw dropped.

"Yes!" Austin shouted beside me, his arms around me again, but my eyes remained fixed on the letters next to the score on the screen.

PB. Personal best. We expected that one since technically, this was our first-ever senior competition.

CR. Canadian record. That one was a little harder to process. No Canadian team had ever received a better mark for a free dance, and we got it for the program that I created.

"Only two points shy of a new world record," the announcer added, and finally, it hit me.

We were the Canadian champions. We just had the best skate of our lives, both of us, and we'd be going to the Olympics in one short month. Austin pulled me to my feet so we could wave to the crowd, and that time, I didn't hear a single boo. If there were any, the cheers drowned them out.

And the best part of all? The man that crowd was cheering for, the man of my dreams, would be in my bed again that night.

All my dreams were finally coming true.

~**Austin**~

Certain moments in my life stayed crystal clear in my memory even years later. The first time I skated with Amy. That ill-fated night I kissed her after the house party. The first time I stepped onto a podium at a world championship.

I already knew this night would be right up there with them.

Amy and I stood next to each other on the podium, bending our necks to receive our gold medals, and when she glanced back at me, nothing but joy on her face, I wanted to capture that look and the way it made me feel and hold onto it forever.

I might have won competitions before, but this one felt different. Being with Amy made it better, simple as that.

Ben waited for us when we got off the ice to do a live interview, broadcast not only on TV but on the jumbotron in the arena too.

"Is there anyone in particular you'd like to thank?" he asked Amy after congratulating us on our win.

"Our coach has worked just as hard as we have these past few months," she said, giving credit where it was very much due. "He believed in us when other people would have said we were crazy. And the support we've received here from the fans has been incredible."

She exaggerated, obviously, given the booing that had thrown us so much earlier in the week, but the crowd ate up her words, roaring in approval while she waved up at them. With her brilliant skating that night, she'd completely won them over.

Ben turned to me. "Do you think an Olympic medal next month is within reach?"

"Honestly? If we skate the way we did tonight, it's inevitable."

I believed that with every fibre of my being.

Once we finally got away to change out of our costumes and pack up all our things, we found Brian waiting for us by the exit.

"I've had a request from your parents. They'd like you to join them in the hotel restaurant when you get back, if you're up to it."

"Which parents?" Amy asked, sounding just as confused as I felt. Mentioning my mom and Amy's mom in the same breath felt wrong. They never liked each other, and as far as I knew, they hadn't spoken in years.

"All of them," Brian confirmed. "They're all having a drink together, so it's up to you if you want to join them."

Amy and I exchanged slightly stunned glances, but I could sense her curiosity. "I guess we could make a quick stop," I suggested, and she nodded. If we didn't, we'd drive ourselves crazy wondering about it.

By the time the taxi pulled up to the hotel, our curiosity had only grown. Hand-in-hand, we walked into the restaurant to find my mom, Amy's dad and his new wife, along with her mom, all sitting around a table together, drinking and talking comfortably.

"Is this a dream?" I asked Amy under my breath. "We haven't been asleep this whole time, have we? We really did just win that event?"

She laughed back. "I think so. Do you want me to pinch you to make sure?"

Reaching behind me, she squeezed my butt cheek, making me jump and causing her to laugh harder. "Very funny," I told her, trying not to smile. "You're going to pay for that later."

For the moment, we made our way over to the table where conversation died off as they saw us approaching.

"Mom," I greeted my mother coolly. I hadn't laid eyes on her since we got back from Tokyo two months earlier. The next person at the table, I greeted more warmly. "Mr Gardiner."

Amy's dad offered me a kind, welcoming smile, and his wife nodded at me. We'd never been introduced and no one seemed to be in any hurry to do so. Instead, all eyes were on me as I turned to Amy's mother. My mouth opened to say hello, but no words came out. Looking into her eyes, I could only picture the last time I saw her, standing in the hospital hallway outside Amy's room when she told me to go away and not come back until Amy asked to see me.

As if she were right there with me, Mrs Wilson stood up and came over to me, tears dotting her eyes. "Austin, I'm so sorry for what I said to you all those years ago. I know it doesn't make it better, but I am truly sorry. I never meant for things to get as out of hand as they did."

My throat closed up, words still refusing to push their way through, but I nodded in acknowledgement of her apology. She was right: it didn't make it better, but I appreciated her saying it anyway.

"How did you all get in touch?" Amy asked, taking the focus off me, to my relief.

"Cynthia reached out to me," Amy's mom answered, turning to look at her. "We realized we've both made some bad choices over the years and we're going to try to do better."

My mom actually owned her mistakes? That seemed next to impossible, but to my shock, she also stood and came over, standing in front of Amy the same way Amy's mom had addressed me. My arm slid around Amy's waist protectively.

"I've had a lot of time in the last few months to think over everything," she said, glancing at me but speaking mostly to Amy. "Talking to your mom has helped me to understand things better than I did before. I know you have every right to hate me, but I just wanted to say thank you for stepping in to skate with Austin. Thank you for helping him to reach his dream even after everything I did to keep you two apart."

In a year that had yielded more surprises than I could have ever imagined, that might have been the single most shocking thing I'd heard. From the tightness in Amy's shoulders, I could tell she wasn't ready to forgive and forget yet any more than I was, but she nodded as I had, acknowledging that at least my mom had made an effort.

"Do you two want to join us?" my mom asked, gesturing back at the table. "We're toasting to your success."

I glanced at Amy again, and when her head shook, I breathed out a sigh of relief. Although I didn't want to stay, I would have if she wanted to. Thankfully, we were on the same wavelength yet again.

"I don't think so," I replied. "But maybe we can do this after the Olympics instead."

Everyone smiled, now that our trip to the Olympics had been confirmed, and after saying goodnight, Amy and I made our way upstairs back to her room.

"I think I've officially experienced everything now," Amy said as we walked into the room. "Winning the gold medal, I might have anticipated, but I could have never imagined that Cynthia Black would actually *thank* me."

I exhaled a deep breath, my mind still spinning from the unexpected detour. "That was pretty surreal alright, but I don't think you've experienced *everything* yet."

Her eyebrows shot up curiously. "What do you mean? What could be left?"

I grinned at her, ready to put everything else out of my mind now that we were alone again. "How about making love to me with that gold medal around your neck?"

Amy laughed as I pulled her to me and any thoughts of our parents or the past or anything outside of that room faded away until all that remained was the love we had for each other.

I had been right the night before when I told her being with her was better than any gold medal. But having both at the same time? *That* really was the best.

Chapter Twelve

~Amelia~

Austin grabbed my hand as we headed out the door of the practice rink in Lausanne. "Let's send our skates back to the hotel with Brian. There's somewhere I want to take you."

We had just finished our second-last practice at the Olympics before the competition started and so far, it had been everything I'd dreamed it would be. We arrived in the city the week before and attended the Opening Ceremony with the whole Canadian Olympic team, hundreds of athletes from different sports. The hockey players towered over me, the snowboarders were cooler than I could ever dream of being, and the sliding sport athletes awed me with their fearlessness. The sense of camaraderie truly gave me the sense of being part of a team, of something bigger than just Austin and me, and knowing that some of them would be at the arena cheering us on while we competed gave us an added lift.

Despite all that, we'd made the decision not to stay in the athletes' village. We wouldn't have been allowed to share a room there, and after that night together at Canadians, we hadn't spent a single night apart. Breaking that streak right before the biggest competition of our lives didn't make any sense.

Austin continued to find new and creative ways to put my flexibility to good use, and I'd been looking forward to more of the same that night, but when he looked down at me with that sweet smile on his face and said he wanted to take me out instead, I couldn't refuse.

"Where are we going?"

The taxi he arranged took us out of the city, up onto one of the surrounding hills until we stopped outside a beautiful, traditional-looking Swiss chalet perched on the hillside. Twinkling lights strung across an outside deck, along with overhead heaters and warm blankets to wrap up in, complementing the breathtaking view over Lake Geneva.

"It'll be dark pretty soon but we can enjoy the view while it lasts," Austin said as we took a seat at the table he'd reserved for us.

With the competition coming up, we couldn't go overboard with food, but my stomach growled as the waiter placed a small cheese fondue pot in front of us.

"Let me," Austin offered, picking up a piece of bread and dipping it into the melted cheese. Reaching across the table, he popped it into my open mouth, smearing a small bit of cheese against my lips.

"So good," I groaned before returning the favour, dipping another piece of bread into the cheese and holding it out for him. When he leaned forward to take it between his teeth, I purposefully rubbed it against his cheek before feeding it to him.

His dark eyes sparkled in amusement. "You want to play that game, do you?"

By the time the waiter brought the next course, we both had to use our napkins to scrub cheese off our faces, trying not to giggle.

We sampled a bit from all of the traditional Swiss dishes, talking and laughing while we ate, and every time I looked over at Austin, his eyes gleamed with something I couldn't quite define.

"What?" I finally asked after the tenth time I caught him staring. "Do I still have cheese on my face somewhere?"

"Maybe a little right here," he teased, dipping his finger in the cheesy pasta on the table and wiping it across my cheek. I glared at him before wiping my face clean yet again, but my stern expression melted into a smile when he took my hand and gave it a kiss, both of us leaning towards each other in unison.

"This is the last time we'll be out together before we're Olympic champions," he said, tucking a stray strand of hair behind my ear. "My last time on a date with plain old Amy Gardiner."

"Mia Wilson," I reminded him with a shake of my head. "Are you really never going to call me by my new name?"

"Never. You'll always be my Amy."

Admiration and possessiveness bled through his words, melting my heart. The winter sun had set, and the lights surrounding us reflected in the depths of his eyes as he stared into mine.

I had to change the subject before my emotions overwhelmed me. "Let's not get ahead of ourselves on the Olympic champion thing. The competition hasn't even started yet."

The month since Canadians had been a whirlwind. Along with the training that took up most of our time, we had other obligations too, including media appearances and team events. A couple of days after we won in Ottawa, one of the big national papers ran an exclusive interview with Grace where she finally cleared up the misunderstanding about her earlier remarks. She explained that her decision to take the medication in Tokyo had been partly motivated by her insecurities around me and the attention focused on me, but that I had played no direct part in her decision. The article came across as very sympathetic to her while also being supportive of me and Austin and our Olympic hopes.

It came as no surprise to me to see the byline: Ben Miller, of course.

"Which part of the competition are you looking forward to the most?" Austin asked me, still holding onto my hand with one of his as he rested his head on the other one, his elbow propped up on the table.

The expected answer would be the moment that we won or the moment that we got our medals, but it wouldn't be the truth. I had always preferred beginnings to endings.

"I'm looking forward to taking our starting positions for the rhythm dance, before we've taken a single step, when anything is still possible."

He smiled at me, his dimple nearly making me lose track of the entire conversation.

"What about you?" I asked.

"The second the music stops at the end of our free dance," he answered without hesitation. "Before the marks, before we know what the judges thought. That moment with just you and me, where we'll know in our hearts if we deserve to win it or not."

We took a few minutes to admire the night sky, all the stars twinkling above the hills and the lake, before getting in the taxi and heading back to our hotel.

The next day was our final practice, the last chance to run through the rhythm dance before performing it on the biggest stage of our lives. Each step seemed to float across the ice as we danced together, all the work of the past three months paying off in spades.

We were ready for anything, it felt like, until we stepped off the ice and saw two familiar faces waiting for us, one that we were expecting and one that we definitely weren't.

Ben greeted us with a warm smile before gesturing to the woman behind him. "Is it okay if Grace says hello?"

My eyes immediately went to Austin, unsure how he would feel about that. He hadn't really talked to her since Tokyo, and even after the article came out and she cleared things up, she remained a sensitive subject for him.

He met my gaze and I shrugged, trying to let him know that I would back him up whatever decision he made.

"Sure," he finally gritted out, squaring his shoulders in preparation.

Ben turned to Grace, standing several feet away and clenching her hands nervously, and motioned for her to come over.

"Hi," she said as she joined us, her eyes darting between me and Austin. "You guys look great out there."

Knowing first-hand how painful it was to watch Austin skate with someone else, I couldn't imagine she found that easy to say. Clearly, she was making an effort.

"Thanks, Grace." Austin gave her a tight but sincere smile. "It's good to see you. Can I ask why you're here though?"

Nothing about the question sounded accusatory. He was simply curious.

"I'm here with Ben." She gave the man beside her a surprisingly warm smile. "He's been a really good friend to me since we spoke for the article. We've been in touch ever since. Anyway, I wanted to thank you for texting me at Christmas and checking in on me. I wanted to reply, but... well, I wasn't in a very good place at the time."

I could only imagine, knowing what I went through when I couldn't skate for a while. It sucked that my good fortune in skating with Austin came at the expense of her dream, but sometimes, life simply dealt us cards that weren't fair. I was glad to know she was coming to terms with it in her own way.

Austin seemed to recognize that too, his tone softening. "I understand, and we appreciate your support. Maybe we could all get a drink together when this is all over."

Grace's shoulders visibly relaxed and Ben beamed at her.

"That would be great," she agreed. "Thank you."

They walked away together, his arm slipping around her waist as they went, and Austin shook his head. "Hopefully that's the biggest surprise we get during this competition."

"At this point, I wouldn't rule anything out," I said with a laugh. "But I have a feeling that no matter what, it's all going to go our way. Wait and see."

~Austin~

Amy's body felt tense beside me as we warmed up for our rhythm dance. Nobody else would notice, but I could see it in the way she glanced over her shoulder at the crowd in the Olympic area and the way the corners of her mouth twitched when we approached the centre of the ice.

Given the rather disastrous start we'd had to this program at the Canadian championships, her nerves made complete sense to me, and I took it as my job to help ease them.

"Look at me," I said, tightening my grip around her waist as we circled the ice.

She did, looking up at me curiously, with just a hint of caution. That caution was what I needed to erase.

"Nothing that happened before matters right now. This is the one that everyone's going to remember."

Her lips stopped twitching and curled up into a smile. "I should really charge you rent, since you seem to be living in my head."

"I know you, Amy," I pointed out, placing a quick kiss on her temple. "And I know that you've got this. *We've* got this. Skate it for me, okay? No one else."

By the time we stepped out onto the ice for real, her hesitation had disappeared. We took our starting position and her words from our dinner a couple of nights earlier came back to me: *anything is still possible*. I whispered those words back to her on the ice, feeling the weight of thousands of eyes on us, and when she winked back at me, I knew deep in my heart we were about to ace that dance.

And we did.

With each step, we showed the whole world that our connection, once broken, had been completely restored. We fit together, complementing each other in every way, lifting each other to new heights and pushing each other to a better performance.

Two and a half minutes later, the crowd leapt to their feet and I pulled Amy to me in a tight embrace. Relief and anticipation and joy surrounded us along with the roar of the crowd, and I whispered into her ear: "One more. One more dance just like that and we've got it."

In the kiss 'n' cry area, we watched the marks come up. They were an improvement on our marks for that dance at Canadians, and at that point in the competition, we were in the lead. However, the world champions from the previous year still had to skate.

"Do you want to stay and watch the rest of the teams?" Brian asked, but Amy and I both shook our heads. Our presence there wouldn't make a difference one way or the other, and we needed to stay focused on our own game.

When we were changed and ready to head back to the hotel, he gave us an update.

"The French team is in first."

Disappointment stabbed at my chest, but only for a second. We still had the free dance to go; nothing had been settled yet. "How far are we behind?"

"Less than half a point."

Amy exhaled in relief, understanding the significance of that as much as I did. In dance, that was nothing. We were practically even, meaning everything would come down to the free dance. Amy's dance.

The way it always should have.

Almost before I knew it, we returned to the arena the following day for the second and final part of the competition. Dressing in my soldier's uniform costume, my excitement outweighed any nervousness I felt. I couldn't *wait* to get out there and show off Amy's incredible program. Once we skated it in front of the world that day, everyone would know what I always had: Amy was the best.

Through the luck of the draw, we were the last team to skate. That meant that as soon as our marks came up, we would know how we finished, but I had a feeling we'd know even before that. Our program was more technically challenging than the French team's, so as long as we skated it to its full potential, we would win.

"This is surreal, isn't it?" Amy asked as we stood in the corridor leading to the ice, waiting for the French team to finish skating. We could hear the cheering of the crowd but we did our best to tune it out, focusing only on each other. "We've been working towards this our whole lives, you especially, and it all comes down to four and a half minutes."

"It's crazy," I had to agree. "Are you nervous?"

After thinking about it for a minute, she shook her head. "No. Is that weird? I'm excited to go out there, but I'm not scared."

"It's not weird at all."

We walked towards the ice as the French team took their bows, and the crowd's standing ovation confirmed they'd skated well.

"Good job," I said as we crossed paths with them, and they nodded in acknowledgement, their faces showing relief and pride and hope.

Hope that I had every intention of crushing when we won instead of them.

Amy and I stepped onto the ice, and suddenly, the rest of the world disappeared. The crowd, the judges, the TV cameras, the Olympic logos on the board, all of it vanished from my view. All I could see was the two of us and the ice beneath us, all the days of training, all the nights of longing, all the time apart and all the time together, colliding and compressing into this one moment that we would share and remember forever.

As the other team's marks were announced, we skated to the centre of the ice and stood facing each other. I bent down, leaning my forehead against hers as we took three calming breaths, synchronizing our breathing. "We're going to win this," I whispered to her.

"I love you, Austin," she whispered back, and my heart skipped a beat.

We hadn't said those words yet, though I knew how I felt and I'd been pretty sure she felt them too. Hearing them out loud had to be the most beautiful thing I'd ever heard.

Before I could reply, however, our names were called and I lost my chance to say it back. The eyes of the whole world were on us, and it would have to wait.

We took our starting positions as silence descended like a curtain around us, and when the music started, a sense of stillness and calmness came over me, unlike anything I'd ever felt before.

I would have almost called it an out-of-body experience, except that I was more aware of my body than I ever had been before.

Every tiny sensation registered, every touch of Amy's hand on me and every breath of wind created as we flew down the ice. The crowd blurred in the background, like an impressionist painting, and no sound penetrated my ears except the music and the beating of my heart.

I couldn't hear Amy's heart, but I knew it beat in time with mine, just as in tune with each other as every other part of us.

Every edge was perfect, every step in time and together, every position hit exactly right. The emotion and drama of the program poured out of me, leaving nothing behind.

We had never skated the program better and, as the music ended, I didn't have a single doubt in my mind.

We won. Every cell in my body told me so.

But when I lifted Amy up from her final position and saw the love shining from her eyes, I knew that winning the medal I'd always dreamed of was only the second-most important thing in my life.

"I love you, too," I told her, grabbing her around the waist and kissing her hard for all the world to see.

~**Amelia**~

Having the best moment of your life captured on film for you to replay and rewatch as many times as you like felt a little strange. But no matter how many times I watched our dance, seeing it from the outside like everyone else had, it never replaced the memory of standing on that ice, the crowd cheering for us as Austin took me in his arms and kissed me like his life depended on it.

In the video, the kiss only lasted a few seconds, but in that moment, it felt eternal. It felt like time had stopped, like past, present and future had merged, and the only thing in the world that mattered was that we were together, finally, as partners and lovers, sharing that moment.

Brian grinned at us when we came off the ice, his smile wider than I'd ever seen it.

"Congratulations," he told us both, giving us each a strong hug. "If they don't give you the marks to win, this place is going to riot."

He didn't have to worry.

The marks came up before we even had a chance to sit down and I couldn't have dreamed anything better.

A new Olympic record.

A new World record.

They were even better than the marks we received at Canadians, and we were officially declared the Olympic gold medalists.

The rest of the night passed in a flurry of activity and emotions. We did our post-skate interview with Ben, whose broad smile mirrored ours.

We got our medals, standing on the podium while the national anthem played. I couldn't keep from crying, but I wasn't alone. Austin's eyes were rimmed with red as he alternated between watching the flag being lifted and watching me. We both sang along, out of tune and not even caring.

Not all of it was glamorous. We had to do the doping tests and speak to dignitaries who wanted to congratulate us. By the time we were finally changed and ready to go back to the hotel, I had completely lost track of time, but as my fingers rested on the medal still around my neck as we sat in the taxi, I knew it really didn't matter.

I had everything I needed, and everything I ever wanted.

For the rest of the Games, we simply enjoyed ourselves, having an absolute blast. We went to as many events as we could, cheering on the Canadian hockey players, skiers, curlers and speed skaters. We had drinks with Ben and Grace as we'd promised, as well as with my friends Gaby, Rosa and Jenna who had flown over during their reading week at university to cheer us on.

We even met up with our parents. Austin's mom gave me a hug, which nearly made me faint in shock. Austin told me afterwards that she finally seemed to have accepted that I wasn't going anywhere, so she knew that if she wanted to be a part of his life at all, she'd have to make peace with me.

I sat down with my mom for the first time in person since she told me the truth about what happened with Austin. It had been weighing on my heart that we were so distant, and although I still vehemently disagreed with what she did, the way everything turned out helped to ease my bitterness. Things might not ever be exactly as they had been, but for the first time, it at least seemed possible.

"Mrs Black and I actually have quite a lot in common," she admitted, shaking her head at that odd statement. "We're both divorced, we both spent a lot of our lives at ice rinks, and our kids both hate us."

I knew she was partly joking about the last one, so I didn't take it too seriously. "Are you actually friends now?"

"More than that, actually. We're going to go into business together."

I nearly spit out the drink I'd just taken. "What? What kind of business?"

She shrugged. "We're not sure yet, but we're both pretty determined when we set our mind to something. I think it could work."

Life sure did take some funny turns sometimes. Some of them could break you, but others healed you in ways you never imagined.

On the last day of the Games, we got to my favourite part of any major competition: the figure skating Gala.

All the skaters who placed in the top five of each event got to skate an additional program for the crowd, just for fun. Skaters often used this as a chance to be silly or creative or a little more daring than they could be during the regular competition.

At Canadians, we simply performed our free dance again, not having had the time to work on anything else, but when it came to the Olympics, there had never been a question about which program we were going to skate.

"This is definitely not the way I imagined skating this program for the first time in front of a crowd," I told Austin as we waited by the boards, limbering up for our turn on the ice.

"I can't think of a better way," he replied, smiling at me with all the love I could possibly wish for. "They're going to love it."

We stepped onto the ice as the announcer called our names and waved to the crowd as they cheered. We took our starting positions, and the opening strains of "Goodbye Until Tomorrow" filled the air, the program I created for us to skate together four years earlier, the one the world never got to see, until that night.

As we skated, as the music flowed through us, I felt more connected with the past than ever before. I could see Austin on the ice at 16 years old, the day we first skated together. I could feel his hand in mine the first time we skated this program at the rink in Ottawa. And I could hear his voice the day he asked me to skate it with him again that cold morning in Toronto, just four months before, when we found each other again.

That day, I could have never imagined that we would be performing as Olympic champions together just four months later. It would have seemed too outlandish, too ridiculous to even imagine.

And yet, as Austin smiled down at me while we performed the steps I put together for us all those years ago, I couldn't help feeling that somehow, it was always meant to be.

Epilogue

~**Amelia**~

Six months to the day after Austin and I won our Olympic medals, we stood together in front of a very different crowd as our closest friends, family and colleagues gathered to celebrate our wedding.

Austin proposed on the holiday we took at the end of the skating season. After the World Championships, we were invited to join a professional show that would tour the country. It would take up almost two months of our time, especially since I'd been asked to help choreograph the group numbers, so Austin insisted that we take some time away to ourselves first.

On the beach in St Lucia, far away from any kind of ice except the cubes in our drinks, he got down on one knee as the sun set in the distance.

"Are- are you serious?" I stammered, not sure if I wanted to laugh or cry as he pulled the beautiful, sparkling ring out of his pocket.

"I've never been more serious." He smiled up at me as he reached for my hand. "I don't know exactly when I fell in love with you. I can't name a day or a place, it didn't come on all at once, but eventually, I knew that my life wouldn't feel right without you in it. And then, you were gone."

A pang of regret ran through me, as it always did at the thought of all the time we'd spent apart, both of us hurting. However, that feeling of loss was weaker than it used to be. Each new day with Austin helped to heal the pain of the past and hopefully, with time, it would hardly sting at all.

"I've tried living without you," he continued. "For four years, I tried my best to move on, but it never felt right. Now that you're back, now that we're together in every way, I don't want to waste any more time. I don't care if people think it's too fast. I love you, Amy, and I want to spend the rest of my life with you. No one could ever be a better partner for me than you are. Will you marry me?"

Knowing what it felt like to waste time and miss out on opportunities, I didn't hesitate for a second. "I will. Yes, of course I will."

And so, we stood together at the front of the church as the minister spoke to us about overcoming adversity together. There would be challenges, but after everything we'd already been through, as long as we were together, as long as we talked to each other and shared what we were feeling, I truly felt like there was nothing we couldn't handle.

There were no TV cameras to record our every move like there were when we skated, but a camera still snapped quietly in the background, wielded by our official photographer for the day: Paul Miller, the photographer who went with me when I profiled Austin for the magazine, the day we first came back into contact with each other.

Paul was surprised and honoured when I asked him if he would do it.

"I remember the photography lesson you gave me that day on the waterfront. You obviously know what you're doing," I pointed out. The memory made him smile too, and now that I'd brought it up, I couldn't help asking him about the day in order to finally satisfy my curiosity. "Why did you suggest we do that, anyway? Was it a date? Were you interested in me?"

He huffed in amusement. "Of course I was. You're amazing, Mia."

His answer confused me even more. "But you didn't ever say anything, or make any kind of move."

"Because you were very obviously hung up on someone else."

I certainly had been, even if I would have never admitted it to anyone then. I thought I'd gotten over Austin, but I'd been fooling myself all along.

We had the wedding reception at the skating rink where we trained, the place where we'd gotten to know each other again after our time apart. When we danced our first dance, Austin's eyes twinkled down at me. "I think everyone is disappointed we're not doing something a little flashier."

"They can watch us dance on the ice if they want flashy. This is about you and me."

"As it should be." He leaned down and kissed me, and the world around us disappeared again, just like it always did when he had me in his arms.

Love and laughter filled the night. Austin danced with his mother, who was actually managing to both warm up to me and chill out at the same time. Now that Austin and I had retired and she and my mom had gone into business together, she seemed to be finding a much better balance in her life.

Austin and I had agreed between us that we would forgive both of our mothers for the roles they played in our forced separation. They both made mistakes, which they freely acknowledged, acting in what they thought were our best interests, and they both apologized sincerely. They were eager to build new and better relationships with us, and life was too short for holding onto grudges; the only way to move forward was to let go.

We had all learned that lesson.

My dad and his new family were there, along with my friends from university and Grace with her new boyfriend, Ben.

Ben offered to dance with me while Austin led Grace out to the floor. "Who would have guessed we'd all end up here together?" Ben asked with a smile as he looked around at all the people gathered, people from our past and present, from my life as Amy and my life as Mia.

"Definitely not me." Never in my wildest dreams could I have imagined all of this.

Finally, we'd done our best to visit with everyone, and we were eager to go and get our honeymoon started, even if that night, we were only going back to the house that we already shared.

Austin insisted on carrying me across the threshold, his strong arms holding me securely as they had thousands of times before, but he didn't stop inside the door. He carried me all the way up the stairs and to our bedroom, where my dress soon ended up on the floor next to his tux.

"I don't know how, but this keeps getting better," he whispered to me, his lips brushing softly across my forehead. "I think I can't love you any more than I do, and then I do."

"I love you too, Austin." My hands ran across his naked body, pulling him close to me, until there was no space at all between us, until we were moving as one just as we did on the ice. "I always have, and I always will."

~**Austin**~

Three years later

"Just remember, nobody is perfect at this their first time, okay?" I gave the kids in front of me a warm smile. "You're going to fall down, just accept that right now."

Nervous laughter rippled through the group, as well as a bit of bravado from some of the older boys. They thought they'd be able to stay on their feet, that they weren't going to fall like the younger kids did, but they weren't counting on the toe picks.

Sure enough, half an hour later, everyone had hit the ice at least once, and most of them a lot more than that. But they were all having fun anyway, which was the point. None of these kids had ever been on the ice before and for some of them, this might be the only time they'd ever put on a pair of skates. Just maybe, though, there would be one or two who would fall in love with the feel of the ice beneath their blades just like I had, and that one or two would be all it took to make this all worthwhile.

"Okay, take your skates off, let your feet breathe a bit, and we'll head over to the dance studio and try a few moves there," I told them before sending them off the ice.

Before I could head off after them, a familiar voice called out to me from the boards. "Not bad, Black, but your leg extensions are getting a little sloppy. Don't make me call your choreographer on you."

With a wide grin spreading across my face, I turned to see Amy standing there, a bag slung over her shoulder and our three-month-old son, Axel, in her arms.

The name Axel had been my idea. Along with being a skating name, naturally, it also started with A, just like Austin and Amelia.

Our perfect little family.

"You know I'll never complain about my choreographer coming to see me." I gave her a deep, lingering kiss before placing a much gentler one on Axel's tiny forehead. His eyes focused on me and when he smiled, my heart nearly burst with joy as I raised my eyes back to my beautiful wife. "How's your day been?"

"Busy. I sent Brian the feedback he wanted for his new team, and I've had another call from the coach of that junior Russian team that everyone's talking about. She wants me to fly out to Moscow as soon as possible to get started on this year's programs with them."

Three years on from our gold-medal winning performance, Amy's choreography was more in demand than ever, and I couldn't be prouder of her. She still went by Mia professionally: Mia Black.

"I'm up for a trip to Moscow. Axel and I can hang together while you do your work."

"You don't mind taking a bit of time off from the foundation? This is your busy time too."

The start of the skating season always brought a lot of interest, and we had another surge later in the year after the World championships when skating was on TV every night and kids were more interested in trying it for themselves. Just as I'd hoped it would, my foundation drew new people to the sport, kids who might have never considered ice dancing as a possibility or even really been aware that it existed.

We focused primarily on kids in lower-income neighbourhoods and children of immigrants who came from countries where figure skating wasn't well known or understood. In only our second full year of operation, one of the young men I discovered last year had already moved on to train with Brian. He'd be competing in his first novice competition the following month with the partner Brian found for him, and I couldn't wait to go and cheer him on.

"I can make it work," I told Amy. "You two always come first."

She smiled at me tenderly before her attention drifted in the direction of the locker room where the kids were starting to come out in their street shoes, most of them walking a little funny as they adjusted to being on solid ground again.

"What did you think of this group?" she asked. "Any standouts?"

I had a feeling her question wasn't an idle one. "What did you notice?"

She smiled again. "Am I that obvious?"

"Only to me. But seriously, did you see something? I was busy making sure everyone stayed on their feet."

"One girl caught my attention," she admitted. "She stayed by the boards, in the corner, but something in the way that she bent her knees, watching the edges in the ice, moving to the music... it looked like she really felt it."

That did sound promising but I couldn't be sure who she meant. "Come to the dance session," I invited. "You can show me who it is and we'll see how she moves off the ice."

Amy agreed, and I quickly hopped off the ice to take my own skates off before we headed next door to the small dance studio adjacent to the rink. The kids were already there, some of them standing around talking to each other, a few of them chasing each other around the space.

One girl stood to the side, standing in front of the mirror. She looked to be about eleven or twelve years old, and as I watched, she lifted her arm slowly, stretching it out fully to the side as she watched the movement reflected back to her.

I turned to Amy and raised my eyebrows, asking her silently if I had the right girl. She nodded, understanding me completely as usual.

While Amy stayed to the side and watched, Axel sleeping peacefully in her arms, I led the kids through a series of dance exercises. They all took part, but very few took it seriously, with the girl Amy had spotted being an obvious exception.

When the session finished, several of the girls went to coo over the sleeping baby, including the girl that Amy had her eye on. We managed to hold her back when the others left and Amy gave her a warm smile.

"It looks like you like to dance," Amy said, testing out the waters. "How did it feel out on the ice today?"

The girl's cheeks flushed, her eyes still focused on Axel's sleeping face. "It was... different. I didn't know it would feel like that."

"Like what?" Amy prompted.

"Like..." The girl glanced away, searching for the right words. "Like I was connected to it somehow. Like the blades and the ice were working together."

Amy's eyes immediately flew to me and I nodded, in total agreement. That kind of connection couldn't be taught, and though it wouldn't be all she'd need to succeed, it made for a great start.

"What's your name?" I asked.

"Alika," she replied a bit shyly, not looking directly at me.

"Are you interested in taking some skating lessons, Alika?"

"I... don't think my parents can afford that," she answered, her head still bowed.

"That's not a problem. As long as you're interested, we can take care of it."

I gave her brochures with all the information about the foundation's programs and the scholarships available, and told her to have her parents call me if they had any questions. When she left, I returned to Amy and Axel.

"Looks like you might have a new champion on your hands there," Amy said, smiling up at me with an admiration that still took my breath away after all this time.

"I hope so," I agreed. "Too bad this guy's too young to skate with her."

With one finger, I traced a gentle line down Axel's face. He wrinkled his nose adorably, making my heart melt all over again.

"*If* he wants to skate," Amy said, her eyes soft with amusement, "and only if, I'm sure you'll help him find a great partner when the time's right."

"I do have an eye for the best."

My wink made her laugh. "I think you're misremembering. As I recall, *I* chose *you*."

"How about we agree that we chose each other?" I suggested, placing a kiss on her perfect lips. "And that, all things considered, we'd do it again."

"Each and every time," she agreed, giving me a look so full of love, I could hardly handle it.

With all the kids gone, we were alone in the dance studio, and I gently took Axel from her arms and placed him down in his car seat before holding my hand out to my wife. "Dance with me?"

She slid her hand into mine, fitting there just as perfectly as it always had. "There's no music," she pointed out with a teasing smile.

"Hang on."

I left her for only a few seconds so I could pull up a song on the music player. When the opening notes on the piano sounded through the studio, Amy's smile grew bigger and softer at the same time. We'd chosen our wedding song together, and it would always remind me of our story.

I pulled her close to me, her body pressed up against mine, her head resting against my chest as Garth Brooks sang the bittersweet lyrics of The Dance. Every word resonated through me, my soul finally fully healed after all the pain of the past.

Our journey to get there could have been easier, but in the end, I wouldn't have changed it for the world.

~~THE END~~

Bonus Scene

For another glimpse of Amy and Austin's life in the future, you can download a short bonus scene at https://dl.bookfunnel.com/jsb6xafwie

Keep in Touch

For more about my other books and to keep up-to-date with new releases, find all the links here:
https://linktr.ee/melodytyden

www.ingramcontent.com/pod-product-compliance
Lightning Source LLC
Chambersburg PA
CBHW072052110526
44590CB00018B/3140